CAREERS IN THE GRAPHIC ARTS

CAREERS IN THE GRAPHIC ARTS

By

Virginia Lee Roberson

THE ROSEN PUBLISHING GROUP, INC.

New York

Acknowledgments

Thanks To:

My husband, Dave, and sister, Nancy, for their encouragement and continuing support during the writing of this book.

The Talent Pool, Inc., Albuquerque, New Mexico, the graphic arts agency that produced all of the line drawings and illustrative typesetting.

Published in 1988 by The Rosen Publishing Group, Inc.
29 East 21st Street, New York, NY 10010

First Edition

LIBRARY OF CONGRESS
Library of Congress Cataloging-in-Publication Data

Roberson, Virginia Lee
    Careers in the graphic arts .. by Virginia Lee Roberson. — 1st
ed. p. cm.
    Bibliography: p.
    Includes index.
    Summary: Discusses a career in graphic arts, outlining the
educational requirements, training, and skills needed to become an
illustrator, layout artist, designer, or pasteup artist.
    ISBN O-8239-0803-8

    1. Printing industry — Vocational guidance. 2. Graphic arts —
Vocational guidance. [1. Printing industry — Vocational guidance. 2.
Graphic arts — Vocational guidance. 3. Vocational guidance.]
    I. Title.
Z243.A2R58 1988   686.2'023—dc19   88-25146
    CIP
    AC

Manufactured in the United States of America

Contents

49534

About the Author

"I thought my dream of becoming an artist was over when financial circumstances didn't permit me to finish the three-year certificate course in Commercial Art at Pratt Institute. Luckily, though, a number of wonderful employers, through the years, gave me the opportunity to learn and grow," says Virginia Roberson.

Entering Pratt in 1953 with the specific intent of becoming an illustrator, Virginia Roberson didn't find her niche until going to work for her first printer. "I still get a thrill when I watch a piece that I've designed and put together roll off the press," she says. That's my 'baby' being born!"

Progressing from artist to art director to owner of a small graphic arts agency, Virginia Roberson's thirty-year career has been primarily concentrated on the production of camera-ready art for the advertising trade. After years of design, layout, and pasteup of brochures, catalogs, direct mailing pieces, and so on, her desire now is to "semiretire" from the graphic arts field and have a little more time for her other two loves—free-lance writing and her six young grandchildren.

Part 1

Chapter **1**

Heading in the Right Direction

You are a creative person. How do I know that? Simple. You wouldn't have decided to become an artist without the certainty that you possess a good imagination and, moreover, have confidence in your ability to communicate those imaginings. More than likely, that communication takes place on paper—you draw, or paint, or both.

Having this native talent undoubtedly augurs well for a career somewhere in the art field. But *where* in the art field? Perhaps you are reading this book because you have already eliminated the prospect of becoming a fine artist and have chosen to pursue some area of commercial art.

Though many of the topics discussed in the book and most of the advice given would be pertinent to any beginning artist, it is necessary to zoom in on one particular area of commercial art —graphic arts.

Advertising makes the world go 'round by persuading people to buy products and services. Can you picture yourself working in this exciting field, helping merchants to better sell their wares because of your creativity and technical expertise? Can you picture yourself receiving congratulations for an ad you conceived and executed that sold a million thingamabobs for your employer's biggest client? I'll bet you can.

Advertising is everywhere. Turn on the TV, the radio. Open a magazine, a newspaper. Drive down the road a few miles and there's a billboard. Someone has to create and produce all that your eyes encounter in the way of advertising. Why not you?

Now we've narrowed down the career choices. Or have we?

Within the field of graphic arts, what will your job title be? Will you be an illustrator? A designer? A layout or pasteup artist? And where will you seek employment? This book will attempt to illuminate a few of the options, steer you away from the pitfalls, give some technical instruction, and, in general, get you aimed in the right direction. The author, having received little or no guidance, headed off in a totally wrong direction.

I completed only one year of a three-year certificate course at a top school for commercial art in New York. Funds for the second and third years couldn't be raised. That was a pity, for the first year equipped me to do nothing at all! It was a smorgasbord of courses; a sampler of classes, each leading to a different specialty. Based on marks received throughout the year in the various courses, a counselor would then advise the second-year student which career field he or she would be best suited for. The second and third years were devoted to specialization in the recommended field. As I said, I never got that far.

One year of schooling. One portfolio of college work that pointed in no particular direction. No idea of what jobs were even available out there, but because I could draw and desperately needed a job, I assumed that I was meant to be an illustrator.

I presented myself to a local publisher of children's educational books, sans portfolio, and inquired as to the possibility of employment as an illustrator. My naiveté was unbelievable. Instead of laughing at me, however, this warm, grandfatherly publisher asked me if I would be willing to fill several blank sheets of paper with sketches of children. Drawings of little children were my forte, and I walked out with a contract to do the illustrations for two paperback teaching manuals. Thirty or forty pen and ink drawings later, however, I was out of work. The next series of books that required illustration were way beyond my expertise and, luckily, I had sense enough to know it. Perhaps if I had been able at that point to get more training in illustrative techniques and had brushed up on perspective drawing, I might have "made it." I'm inclined to think not, however, as it all turned out. My short-lived career as an illustrator was simply a fluke: having a modicum of talent and being in the right place at the right time.

The next five years found me employed in several jobs that could be said to be related to the art field: silk-screen cutter, ink-tracer of schematics and wiring diagrams, and, later, layout of schematics and wiring diagrams from engineering roughs. I felt that I was just biding my time until an illustration job that I could handle came along.

I might have remained frustrated and slightly bored for many more years if my niche hadn't come looking for *me*. A friend-of-a-friend had just started a small printshop and was looking for an "artistic" person whom he could teach the rudiments of layout and pasteup. It sounded like much more fun than what I was doing and an opportunity to learn something new. In barely a month I knew that I had found my niche. This work encompassed a broad range of skills and abilities I hadn't realized I possessed. Drawing or sketching, while helpful on many occasions, seemed to be secondary to other abilities needed to be successful.

Let's examine a few of those important, but seldom considered at the outset, skills you will need at your command:

1. Eye-hand coordination. Steady hands. Assuming that you draw, this ability is probably already well developed.
2. Organizational skills. You're given several galleys of type and a bushel basket of photos with the instruction, "Now put together a terrific brochure!" Knowing how and where to start making sense of these components is absolutely necessary. Whether illustrator, designer, or layout or pasteup artist, you need organizational ability to a very high degree. Organize your *thinking* first; the rest should follow automatically.
3. Concentration. Attention to detail. If your mind wanders easily, you might make an error in measurement or leave out a component, thus ruining a job. Without concentration, mistakes are easy to make and often too costly for the employer to consider keeping you on. In other words, no Space Cadets allowed!
4. Neatness. Are you always neat in your work habits? No need to work in white gloves, but dirty fingerprints or a glob of rubber cement left on a completed piece distinguish the

amateur from the professional. Neat, clean work tells your employer, also, that you care about what you're doing.

5. Ability to work well under pressure. The field of graphic art is full of deadlines. You are apt to be given an absolutely unrealistic time frame in which to complete a project. Either the adrenalin flows and you slip into high gear, or you crack. You're in great shape if you enjoy the challenge of performing "miracles." You won't last long if you don't.

Granted, most of the foregoing skills or abilities would be desired of any employee, regardless of profession. The nature of the work in graphic art, however, *demands* these attributes. If you can honestly say that your repertoire includes all of them, you may well enjoy a large lead over your competition for a particular job slot. An employer likes to hear, "I work well under pressure. Tight deadlines don't faze me," or, "My ability to organize a job is one of my best qualities." If you feel a little weak in any area, strengthen it before taking that first interview.

End of lecture. It's time to consider in what direction you might like to head. Without a little understanding of what a particular job is all about, it's difficult to make choices. So we'll look briefly at four "artist" positions from a specialization point of view, although more often than not small companies would require a combination of skills.

Illustrator

The illustrator provides original, finished drawings or paintings for brochures, ads, catalogs, billboards, storyboards, and so on. Illustrators usually, though not always, specialize within the craft. Three specialties that come quickly to mind are: fashion illustrator, hard-line illustrator (furniture, appliances, autos, etc.), and cartoonist. A mastery of several media and working knowledge of how to prepare for print or TV are a must. Ability with an airbrush would be a large feather in your cap.

Illustrators are employed by the larger advertising agencies and by retail businesses with in-house art departments whose products are so rapidly changing that illustrations are updated daily, weekly, or monthly.

A number of companies across the U.S. mass-produce books or original illustrations called clip art. The books are sold to small businesses that do not employ a full-time illustrator but need generic illustration from time to time. Clip art producers hire illustrators who have styles and techniques that have proven salable.

With an exceptional portfolio, you might approach smaller advertising agencies, graphic art agencies, or TV studios on a freelance basis. Building a stable of many clients who call on you now and then to supply illustration can be highly lucrative in the long run. Book publishers also sometimes use free-lancers for the illustrative work they require.

A word of warning: There is little room for a mediocre illustrator. Better shoot for top-notch—or else list illustration as a sideline ability when seeking employment.

Layout Artist

The layout artist takes the known (and often just guessed at) components of a piece of advertising and organizes them into a well-designed, functional, and smoothly flowing unit. The talents of the layout artist overlap with those of the designer, as the basic elements and rules of good design must be employed. The layout artist may lay out (design) the area for something as small as a business card or as large as a 48-page (or more) catalog. In many cases a *rough layout* executed in pencil is all that is required to give the pasteup artist an idea of where the various components will be placed. At other times a *comprehensive layout* in marker, colored pencil, or color key material is needed. The comprehensive layout is intended to look as much as possible like a finished, printed piece. Clients (usually those with little imagination) may ask to see a comprehensive layout of an advertising piece before type is set or any other work is started. In general, the layout artist conceptualizes the finished piece and executes his or her ideas on paper in one or more of the media mentioned. Organizational skills are certainly the keyword here.

Good layout artists should always be in demand by advertising agencies, graphic art agencies, large department stores and other retail businesses with in-house art departments, printers with art departments, newspapers, and utility companies that handle their own promotion with in-house art and printing capabilities.

We have looked at layout as a specialty, but you should know that it is most often combined with pasteup as a job description. Artists I have hired over the past two decades were expected not only to do layout but follow through with the pasteup on their assigned pieces. Only a very large firm would be able to make the two functions discrete.

Designer

The work of the designer overlaps with layout in many areas. Indeed, the job descriptions are often used interchangeably. Most designers must lay out their ideas on paper, making them, immediately, layout artists. A layout artist, however, may not be capable of certain design tasks such as creating a logo (company trademark or identifier) or typography design (creating a new typeface). Any original pattern or device used in graphic art is the province of a designer.

In my own differentiation, the person who designs a particular *space* (whether column, panel, or page) is essentially doing "layout." When he or she is *creating something* where formerly there was nothing, that person is a "designer."

Designers or design/layout artists should expect to find employment in the same types of companies listed for layout artists.

Pasteup Artist

The pasteup artist takes all the components of a particular piece—galleys of type, photos and/or illustrations, border devices, and logo—and pastes them with an adhesive on paper or board in exactly the position and relationship to one another prescribed by the layout.

This is where several of the skills/abilities mentioned earlier come into play: neatness, concentration, and the ability to work well under pressure. A neat, accurate pasteup artist is vital to any organization in the graphic arts field. One element that was not mentioned is *speed*. Add "fast" to accurate and neat, and you would seldom be unemployed. Any two qualities, however, without the third leaves something lacking from an employer's point of view. One exception: A prospective employer realizes that speed comes with practice and might be patient with an inexperienced pasteup artist for a while in lieu of paying a higher salary.

We have looked at pasteup as a specialty, but again chances for employment are greatly increased with the additional ability of layout. The person who can look at a blank space and visualize the placement of components without first doing a rough is especially valuable.

A pasteup artist (particularly one with good layout skills) can find employment with any of the agencies or businesses previously mentioned.

I realize that you want to be an artist, not a copywriter or typesetter, so I will discuss those jobs only briefly.

The copywriter writes the words (copy) necessary to describe the client's product or service. He or she has a creative, thematic approach to selling the product or service and is responsible for coming up with a "grabber," lead-in words or headlines that will make the intended audience pay attention and want to know more.

A small agency, like the one I owned for five years, seldom has the need or the budget for a full-time copywriter. We had no copywriter per se, but three of us did write copy. If you find employment in a small agency and have a flair for writing, you might find yourself doing a little copywriting here and there. Try it, you might like it!

The typesetter types (typesets) all the copy in final form (galleys) to be pasted down. The equipment can range from prehistoric to state of the art. Most artists who know how to touch-type could learn to be typesetters. A good typist, strange as it may seem, is not automatically a good typesetter; much of the typesetting equipment available requires the operator to visualize the finished type *before* giving instructions to the machine. Thus, an "artistic" background is helpful.

If you have the opportunity to learn typesetting, take it. As an employer, on one occasion I was seeking a part-time artist and, at the same time, a part-time typesetter (in addition to our full-time typesetter, so that we could extend the production hours on our machine). We hired a woman who was able to do both. She worked mornings as a typesetter and afternoons as pasteup artist. We had to hire only one employee, and she had a full-time job!

I hope at this juncture you have gained some sense of direction and that one of the job descriptions is particularly appealing. I wouldn't advocate being a jack-of-all-trades if it meant being master-of-none, but if you are able to perfect skills in more than one area you are bound to find employment more readily and be of greater value to an employer.

Chapter **11**

Education or OJT?

Now that you have some idea of where you're headed, let's look at the preparation necessary to enter the field. Does it take education or on-the-job training (OJT)? or does it require both?

Unfortunately, the type of apprenticeship so common in medieval days does not exist anymore. No longer can a youth learn his or her craft as an apprentice, working for room and board in lieu of wages. As I'm sure you know, businesses must by law pay employees no less than the current federal minimum wage ($3.35 per hour at this writing). Much of the time it is an "employer's market": one position available and fifty applicants with varying amounts of experience eager to work for that minimum wage. With no training and no education, you will be competing with applicants who have at least a few months of one or both. From an employer's point of view, whom would you hire?

Apprenticeships still exist in a more indirect way, however. Perhaps you're an excellent typist with a winning personality. An ad agency needs a receptionist/typist and no experience is necessary; they will train. It's possible to learn a great deal about the business from this inside position, but you may become frustrated, as I did.

One of the many early jobs I held was "apprentice to the advertising business" (before minimum wage went into effect). Ensconced at the front desk, I had as my primary duties greeting clients, answering phones, and typing copy for radio ads. Occasionally I was asked to "try out" on an ad—either writing copy for a radio spot or doing pasteup for newspaper or magazine advertising. The interruptions were legion: clients in and out, phones ringing constantly, and salemen handing me copy to type that they had to have in a hurry. Seldom could I complete a project I started. Someone would snatch it away from me, giving it to experienced hands to finish because it was due immediately. Frustrated with how little I was learning and the minuscule pay I was earning, I quit after only six months. But you might have more patience than I did—or find a company that will allow you to "try out" more, during the workday or on your own time, while paying you minimum wage for your typist/receptionist work.

A small printshop might hire an inexperienced person to do bindery work, take orders, or run a copier. No matter what the job, with good watching and listening skills you can gain a wealth of usable knowledge. Informing a prospective employer of your future goals and expressing your interest in his or her particular business may help. No employer (that I know of) started at the top. There's usually a soft spot in the boss's heart for the applicant who is eager to learn and willing to come up through the ranks. Apprenticing in this manner is one way, albeit time-consuming, to gain entry into the graphic arts field. It's an alternative you might consider.

Let's hold off on education for a moment and concentrate on the rest of OJT (apprenticing as described above is one kind of on-the-job training). We'll assume at this point that you're not a typist/receptionist or perhaps you don't want employment as something other than an artist. Then what can you do to compete with those applicants who offer a prospective employer at least a minimum amount of experience or education? You can free-lance.

Webster defines a free-lancer as "a writer, actor, etc. who is not under contract for regular work but sells his writing or services to individual buyers."

Free-lancing is often the end of the line: Most artists work in-house for many years as an hourly or salaried employee before becoming an independent contractor. With better-than-average organizational and technical skills, plus an extraordinary ability for self-discipline, they are able to leave the security of steady employment and still earn an enviable living. If free-lancing is usually the end of the line, why am I suggesting this approach to you? Because it can also be a *beginning*—if you are willing to invest lots of time and hard work, with little or no remuneration, and possibly some amount of your own money. How do you get started? Easy.

Everyone has a mother, father, aunt, uncle, sister, brother, friend who belongs to an organization. They are members of a church or temple. They own a small business. Clubs, organizations, churches, temples, and businesses all need artwork from time to time: an ad for the newspaper, a poster, business cards, a letterhead, a flyer. Where could they possibly get their artwork done free? Why, by you, of course. These friends and relatives can be your first "clients." But you'll need to demonstrate that you can do the work they need, even though you expect to donate your time and money for the opportunity to gain experience.

The payoff for you, after all the unpaid labor, will be a portfolio of printed pieces that you can show as examples of your work. No employer will ask you, "Did you do that poster for your Aunt Susie?" The quality of your work will speak for itself.

Later chapters of this book are devoted to the step-by-step instruction that will allow you to start free-lancing. Start *looking* at every printed piece that comes into your home. Begin noticing newspaper and magazine ads. Keep your eyes open for billboards as you're driving. Examine menus closely when eating in a restaurant. Ask for a business card from any salesperson you deal with. Try to absorb the professional appearance that these varied print materials have in common. Do this *before* you sit down and attempt to produce anything. Free-lancing with friends and relatives as clients is another method of entry into the world of graphic art.

Now let's take a look at education. Should you spend the time and money on schooling? If tuition money isn't readily available and you are not a good candidate for financial aid, your decision will be easy: You'll skip the education and become the artist you'd like to be by one of the methods already described. If funds are available, on the other hand, should you enroll for training at a college, university, or technical school? Of course—*but...*

My years of experience as an art director (in charge of hiring and firing) and agency owner (again, with that duty) make me hesitant to hire new graduates without a day or two of paid tryout on the board. Armed with an excellent portfolio and a recent diploma or certificate, they obviously have proven their art ability. They have also become familiar with the lingo or jargon—the trade vocabulary necessary for communication between employer and employee. Then what's the problem? Time.

School projects and homework assignments are sometimes completed over weeks or months. The work in the portfolio has merit, but the business card might have taken three or four days to do; the brochure, two weeks or more. That won't do in the real world. Unless a particular school strives to give students the same fast-paced environment they'll encounter later on, the course will serve only as a basic foundation, not the magic key to a well-paid position.

Taking a good course at a reputable school or institute is certainly worthwhile. Professional constructive criticism is a valuable tool that can be used in perfecting your craft. This is one item that would be lacking if you started out as a free-lancer; friends and relatives may not be able to give *constructive* criticism, only criticism. Be prepared, as a new graduate, though, to start near the bottom of the pay scale. You'll still need work experience to rise to the top.

I am not qualified to rate any school on the excellence of its graphic arts course. The listing that follows is only that—a listing. I have tried to select schools with courses geared to entry into the graphic arts field, eliminating those that seemed too general or aimed at fine art. Also, I have paid attention to geographical location, trying to give every state some representation.

SCHOOLS OF GRAPHIC ARTS

The schools are four-year institutions unless otherwise indicated. Costs shown are for tuition and fees, exclusive of room and board. All figures are for 1986/87 unless otherwise indicated. Projected figures are preceded by *.

Key: A-Associate, C-Certificate, B-Bachelor's, M-Master's, D-Doctorate. R-Resident, OD-Out of District, OS-Out of State.

ALABAMA
Alabama, University of, University
Advertising and Public Relations
B,M $1,254/R $2,690/OS

ARIZONA
Arizona State University, Tempe
Graphic Arts, Commercial Art
   B,M $1,136/R $4,261/OS
Eastern Arizona College, Thatcher
Advertising Design
   A/2-Yr. $416/R $2,744/OS
Maricopa Technical Community College, Phoenix
Commercial Art and Advertising
   C,A   *$548/R   *$3,638/OS
Pima Community College, Tucson
Advertising Art and Design, Graphics Technology
   C,A/2-Yr. $408/R $2,496/OS
ARKANSAS
Southern Arkansas University, Tech., Camden
Advertising and Commercial Art
   A $900/R $1,400/OS
CALIFORNIA
Academy of Art College, San Francisco
Advertising and Graphic Arts
   B,M $4,840
Allan Hancock College, Santa Maria
Graphic Design
   A/2-Yr. $100/R $2,470/OS
American River College, Sacramento
Advertising and Sales
   A/2-Yr. $100/R $2,680/OS
Art Center College of Design, Pasadena
Advertising Art and Design
   B,M $5,948
Bakersfield College, Bakersfield
Graphic Arts
   A/2-Yr. $100/R $2,650/OS
California College of Arts and Crafts, Oakland
Graphic Design
   C,B,M, $6,500
California Polytechnic State University, San Luis Obispo
Graphic and Visual Communications
   B $704/R $4,484/OS
Chabot College, Hayward
Commercial Art
   A/2-Yr. $100/R $2,440/OS
Citrus College, Azusa
Commercial Art
   C,A/2-Yr. $100/R $2,800/OS
Cosumnes River College, Sacramento

Graphic Design
C/2-Yr. $100/R $2,660/OS
Don Bosco Technical Institute, Rosemead
Graphic Communications
A/2-Yr. (Men's) $2,410
Foothill College, Los Altos Hills
Commercial Art
A/2-Yr. $100/R $2,800/OS
Fullerton College, Fullerton
Advertising Design
A/2-Yr. $100/R $2,980/OS
Glendale Community College, Glendale
Advertising Art and Design
C,A/2-Yr. $100/R $2,650/OS
Golden West College, Huntington Beach
Graphic Arts Technology
C,A/2-Yr. $100/R $2,650/OS
Laney College, Oakland
Graphic Arts
C,A/2-Yr. $100/R $2,650/OS
Long Beach City College, Long Beach
Advertising and Display
C,A/2-Yr. $100/R $2,290/OS
Los Angeles Pierce College, Woodland Hills
Advertising Art and Design
A/2-Yr. $100/R $3,220/OS
Los Angeles Valley College, Van Nuys
Commercial Art
A/2-Yr. $100/R $3,010/OS
Moorpark College, Moorpark
Commercial Art, Graphic Arts Communication
A/2-Yr. $100/R $3,010/OS
Mount San Antonio College, Walnut
Commercial Art, Graphics Technology
A/2-Yr. $100/R $2,800/OS
Otis Art Institute of Parsons School of Design, Los Angeles
Graphic and Advertising Design
A $7,130
Pacific Union College, Angwin
Commercial Art
A,B $6,225
Palomar Community College, San Marcos
Graphic Arts
C,A/2-Yr. $100/R $2,650/OS
Pasadena City College, Pasadena

Advertising Art and Design
  A/2-Yr. $100/R $2,800/OS
Rio Hondo College, Whittier
  Commercial Art
  C,A/2-Yr. $100/R $2,680/OS
Riverside City College, Riverside
  Commercial Art
  A/2-Yr. $100/R $2,650/OS
San Diego City College, San Diego
  Commercial Art, Graphic Reproductions
  C,A/2-Yr. $100/R $2,944/OS
San Joaquin Delta College, Stockton
  Commercial Art
  A/2-Yr. $100/R $2,650/OS
San Jose State University—San Jose
  Graphic Design
  B   *$727/R   *$4,507/OS
San Mateo, College of, San Mateo
  Commercial Art
  A/2-Yr. $100/R $2,740/OS
Santa Ana College, Santa Ana
  Commercial Art
  A/2-Yr.   No tuition information available
Santa Barbara City College, Santa Barbara
  Graphic Communications
  C,A/2-Yr. $100/R $2,650/OS
Shasta College, Redding
  Graphic Arts and Advertising
  A/2Yr. $100/R $2,560/OS
Solano Community College, Suisun City
  Commercial Art
  A/2-Yr. $100/R $2,560/OS
Southwestern College, Chula Vista
  Advertising Art and Design
  C,A/2-Yr. $100/R $2,170/OS
Woodbury University, Los Angeles
  Graphic Design
  B $6,120˙
COLORADO
Aims Community College, Greeley
  Graphics Technology
  C/2-Yr. $563/R $923/OD $2,723/OS
Arapahoe Community College, Littleton
  Commercial Art
  C,A/2-Yr. $812/R $2,756/OS

Mesa College, Grand Junction
Graphic Arts, Graphic Communications
A $1,154/R $3,200/OS
CONNECTICUT
Bridgeport, University of, Bridgeport
Graphic Design
B   *$7,850
Connecticut, University of, Storrs
Graphic Design
B $1,937/R $4,827/OS
Hartford, University of, West Hartford
Commercial Art, Graphic Arts
B $8,575
New Haven, University of, West Haven
Graphic and Advertising Design
A,B $6,430
Northwestern Connecticut Community College, Winsted
Graphic Design
A/2-Yr. $632/R $1,796/OS
Western Connecticut State University, Danbury
Graphic Design
B $1,292/R $2,902/OS
DELAWARE
Wilmington College, New Castle
Advertising Art and Design
A   *$3,430
DISTRICT OF COLUMBIA
District of Columbia, University of the, Washington, DC
Commercial Art
A   *$634/R   *$2,494/OS
FLORIDA
Boca Raton, College of, Boca Raton
Commercial Art
A/2-Yr. $6,900
Daytona Beach Community College, Daytona Beach
Commercial Advertising and Art
A/2-Yr. $599/R $1,292/OS
Flagler College, St. Augustine
Commercial Art
B $3,470
Florida Agricultural and Mechanical University, Tallahassee
Graphic Arts Technology
B   '85/'86: $897/R $2,504/OS
Lake-Sumter Community College, Leesburg
Commercial Art

A/2-Yr. $660/R $1,290/OS
Miami-Dade Community College, Miami
Graphic or Commercial Arts, Advertising and Public Relations, Commercial Art Pasteup Apprentice
A,C/2-Yr. '85/'86: $700/R $1,405/OS
National Education Center/Bauder-Brown, Ft. Lauderdale
Commercial Art
A/2-Yr. $4,320
Palm Beach Junior College, Lake Worth
Commercial Art
A/2Yr. '85/'86: $681/R $1,303/OS
Ringling School of Art and Design, Sarasota
Graphic Design
C,B $5,600
Saint Johns River Community College, Palatka
Graphic Design
A/2-Yr. '85/'86: $570/R $1,140/OS
Santa Fe Community College, Gainesville
Graphics Design Techology
A/2-Yr. '85/'86: $747/R $1,494/OS
Valencia Community College, Orlando
Graphic Arts
A/2-Yr. $538/R $1,321/OS
GEORGIA
Art Institute of Atlanta, Atlanta
Commercial Art
A/2-Yr. $5,250
HAWAII
Brigham Young University–Hawaii Campus, Laie
Commercial Art
A $1,560
IDAHO
Boise State University, Boise
Advertising Art and Design
B '85/'86: $1,044/R $2,944/OS
Idaho State University, Pocatello
Graphic Arts
C '85/'86: $1,040/R $2,940/OS
Ricks College, Rexburg
Advertising Design
A/2-Yr. $1,154
ILLINOIS
Bradley University, Peoria
Graphic Design
B *$6,568

Chicago Academy of Fine Art, Chicago
Advertising Art and Design
C,A,B, No tuition information available
City College of Chicago/Kennedy-King College, Chicago
Commercial Art
C,A/2-Yr. $730/R $1,942/OD $2,304/OS
City College of Chicago/Loop College, Chicago
Commercial Art
A/2-Yr. $730/R $1,556/OD $2,305/OS
Dupage, College of, Glen Ellyn
Commercial Art
C,A/2-Yr. $864/R $2,496/OD $3,312/OS
Illinois Central College, East Peoria
Graphic Arts, Graphic Design
A/2-Yr. $795/R $2,441/OD $3,031/OS
Illinois, University of/Urbana-Champaign, Urbana
Graphic Design
B $1,960/R $2,812/OS
Illinois Wesleyan University, Bloomington
Commercial Art
A,B $7,190
MacCormac Junior College, Chicago
Commercial Art
A/2-Yr. $4,050
Thornton Community College, South Holland
Advertising Art and Design
C,A/2-Yr. *$960/R *$1,860/OD *$2,580/OS
Triton College, River Grove
Advertising Art
C,A/2-Yr. $810/R $2,410/OD $3,210/OS
William Rainey Harper College, Palatine
Commercial Art, Graphic Art
C,A/2-Yr. $840/R $1,918/OD $2,571/OS
INDIANA
Anderson College, Anderson
Graphic Design
B $5,280
Evansville, University of, Evansville
Commercial Art
B $6,592
Fort Wayne Art Institute, Fort Wayne
Graphic Design
C,B '84/'85: $1,025
Indiana Univ./Purdue Univ. at Fort Wayne, Fort Wayne
Commercial Art

   A $1,453/R $3,575/OS
Saint Francis College, Fort Wayne
Commercial Art
   A,B $4,192
IOWA
Drake University, Des Moines
Commercial Art
   B $7,130
Hawkeye Institute of Technology, Waterloo
Commercial Art
   A   *928/R   *$1,792/OS
Iowa State University, Ames
Graphic Design
   B $1,390/R $4,080/OS
Iowa Western Community College/Council Bluffs Campus, Council
Bluffs
Graphic Arts
   C/2-Yr.   *$1,110/R   *$2,130/OS
Kirkwood Community College, Cedar Rapids
Graphic Arts
   C/2-Yr.   *$852/R   *$1,704/OS
Upper Iowa University, Fayette
Commercial Art
   A $5,535
KANSAS
Johnson County Community College, Overland Park
Commercial Art
   A/2-Yr.   *$675/R   *$2,160/OS
Marymount College, Salina
Graphic Design
   B $4,230
Pittsburg State University, Pittsburg
Commercial Art
   A   *$1,102/R   *$2,352/OS
Wichita State University, Wichita
Graphic Design
   B,M   *$1,334/R   *$3,244/OS
KENTUCKY
Jefferson Community College, Louisville
Commercial Art
   A/2-Yr. $540/R $1,620/OS
Kentucky, University of/Community College System, Lexington
Commercial Art Technology
   A/2-Yr. $1,332/R $3,812/OS
Morehead State University, Morehead

Graphic Arts Technology
  A $1,070/R $2,950/OS
Northern Kentucky University, Highland Heights
Graphic Design
  B $1,000/R $2,800/OS
LOUISIANA
Delgado Community College, New Orleans
Commercial Art
  A/2-Yr. '85/'86: $570/R $1,250/OS
Louisiana College, Pineville
Advertising Art and Design
  B $2,745
Louisiana State University and Agriculture and Mechanical College,
Baton Rouge
Graphic Design
  B '85/'86: $1,277/R $3,277/OS
Northeast Lousisiana University, Monroe
Advertising Design
  B '85/'86: $988/R $1,868/OS
Northwestern State University, Natchitoches
Advertising Art and Design
  B '85/'86: $1,045/R $1,925/OS
MAINE
Central Maine Vocational/Technical Institute, Auburn
Graphic Arts, Graphic Arts Technology
  A $840/R $1,640/OS
MARYLAND
Columbia Union College, Takoma Park
Commercial Art
  A $6,180
Harford Community College, Bel Air
Advertising and Public Relations
  C,A *$948/R *$1,968/OD *$3,258/OS
Maryland Institute, College of Art—Baltimore
Graphic Design
  B $7,400
Montgomery College, Rockville Campus, Rockville
Advertising Art and Design
  A/2-Yr. '85/'86: $1,155/R $2,085/OD $2,805/OS
MASSACHUSETTS
Boston University, Boston
Graphic Design
  B,M $11,100
Bunker Hill Community College, Charlestown
Graphic and Visual Communication

A/2-Yr. *$835/R *$2,527/OS
Chamberlayne Junior College, Boston
Commercial Art
A/2-Yr. $4,690
Emerson College, Boston
Advertising and Display
B $8,670
Greenfield Community College, Greenfield
Graphic Communication, Graphic Design
A,C/2-Yr. $931/R $2,623/OS
Massachusetts College of Art, Boston
Graphic Design
C,B '85/'86: $1,360/R $3,616/OS
Mount Ida Junior College, Newton Centre
Graphic Design
A/2-Yr. $6,066
Springfield Technical Community College, Springfield
Graphic Arts Technology
A/2-Yr. $869/R $2,561/OS
Swain School of Design, New Bedford
Graphic Design
B *$6,100
Worcester Art Museum, School of The, Worcester
Graphic Arts
C '84/'85: $1,950
MICHIGAN
Alpena Community College, Alpena
Graphic Arts Technology
C,A/2-Yr. $780/R $1,080/OD $1,800/OS
Andrews University, Berrien Springs
Graphic Arts Technology
A,B $6,300
Baker Junior College of Business, Flint
Graphic Design
A/2-Yr. $3,020
Center for Creative Studies/College of Art and Desgin, Detroit
Graphic Design, Advertising Design
C,B $6,120
Ferris State College, Big Rapids
Commercial Art
A $1,671/R $3,318/OS
Gogebic Community College, Ironwood
Commercial Art
A/2-Yr. $690/R $1,050/OD $1,470/OS
Grand Valley State College, Allendale

Advertising and Public Relations
    B $1,502/R $3,590/OS
Kendall School of Design, Grand Rapids
Advertising Design
    C,A   '85/'86: $4,395
Kirtland Community College, Roscommon
Graphic Design
    A/2-Yr.   *$653/R   *$923/OD   *$1,373/OS
Macomb County Community College/South Campus, Warren
Graphics and Commercial Art
    C,A/2-Yr. $960/R $1,515/OD $1,815/OS
Madonna College, Livonia
Commercial Art
    A,B $2,690
Michigan, University of, Ann Arbor
Graphic Design
    B,M   '85/'86: $2,231/R $7,319/OS
Muskegon Community College, Muskegon
Graphic Reproduction Technology
    A/2-Yr.   *840/R   *$1,140/OD   *$1,530/OS
Northern Michigan University, Marquette
Graphic Arts, Graphic Design
    A,B   *$1,556/R   *$3,559/OS
Northwestern Michigan College, Traverse City
Commercial Art
    A/2-Yr. $1,035/R $1,624/OD $1,851/OS
Oakland Community College/Auburn Hills Campus, Auburn Heights
Commercial Art
    A/2-Yr. $780/R $1,170/OD $1,590/OS
Saint Clair County Community College, Port Huron
Advertising Art and Design
    A/2-Yr. $960/R $1,600/OD $1,980/OS
Washtenaw Community College, Ann Arbor
Commercial Artist
    A/2-Yr. $870/R $1,380/OD $1,800/OS
Western Michigan University, Kalamazoo
Graphic Arts
    B   *$1,496/R   *$3,626/OS
MINNESOTA
North Hennepin Community College, Brooklyn Park
Graphic Design
    A/2-Yr. $1,193/R $1,790/OS
Northwestern College, Roseville
Commercial Art
    A,B $5,775

Saint Cloud State University, St. Cloud
  Graphic Design
    B $1,595/R $2,430/OS
Saint Mary's College, Winona
  Graphic Design
    B $6,250
MISSISSIPPI
Jones County Junior College, Ellisville
  Commercial Art
    A/2-Yr. $536/R $576/OD $1,136/OS
Mississippi University for Women, Columbus
  Advertising Art and Design
    B   '85/'86: $1,075/R $2,257/OS
Southern Mississippi, University of, Hattiesburg
  Graphic Arts Communication
    B   '85/'86: $1,429/R $2,611/OS
MISSOURI
Central Missouri State University, Warrensburg
  Graphic Arts Technology
    A,B   '85/'86: $992/R $1,834/OS
Lincoln University, Jefferson City
  Graphic Arts
    B   '85/'86: $806/R $1,612/OS
Northeast Missouri State University, Kirksville
  Commercial Art, Graphic Arts
    C,B   '85/'86: $770/R $1,540/OS
Saint Louis Community College at Florissant Valley, St. Louis
  Advertising Art and Design
    A/2-Yr. $795/R $1,095/OD $1,430/OS
Saint Louis Community College at Meramec, Kirkwood
  Advertising and Commercial Art
    A/2-Yr. $848/R $1,232/OD $1,584/OS
Washington University, St. Louis
  Graphic Design
    B,M $10,572
William Woods College, Fulton
  Commercial Art
    B $6,130
MONTANA
Eastern Montana College, Billings
  Commercial Art
    A   *$981/R   *$2,385/OS
NEBRASKA
Kearney State College, Kearney
  Commercial Art

A $1,079/R $1,694/OS
Metropolitan Technical Community College, Omaha
Graphic and Applied Arts Technology
C,A/2-Yr. $788
NEVADA
Clark County Community College, Las Vegas
Graphic Arts
A/2-Yr. $615/R $2,815/OS
NEW HAMPSHIRE
New Hampshire Vocational/Technical College, Laconia
Graphic Arts
A $1,500/R $3,900/OS
NEW JERSEY
Gloucester County College, Sewell
Graphic Arts
C/2-Yr. *$750/R *$780/OD *$3,780/OS
NEW MEXICO
Eastern New Mexico University/Portales Campus, Portales
Commercial Art
B $895/R $2,980/OS
NEW YORK
Bryant and Stratton Business Institute, Buffalo
Commercial Art
A $3,820
Cazenovia College, Cazenovia
Advertising Art and Design
A/2-Yr. $5,650
Cornell University, Ithaca
Graphic Arts
M,D $11,500
Daeman College, Amherst
Graphic Design
B $5,930
Long Island University/Southampton College, Southampton
Graphic Arts
B *$6,875
New York City Technical College of The City University of New York,
Brooklyn
Graphic Arts
A $1,298/R $2,598/OS
Parsons School of Design, New York
Graphic Design
C,A,B, $8,054
Pratt Institute, Brooklyn
Graphic Design

A $8,150
Queens College of The City University of New York, Flushing
Commercial Art
    B $1,422/R $2,722/OS
Rochester Institute of Technology, Rochester
Graphic Design
    A,B $7,851
Saint Rose, College of, Albany
Advertising and Graphic Design
    B $5,670
State University of New York/Agricultural and Technical College at
Farmingdale, Farmingdale
Advertising Art and Design, Graphic Arts
    A/2-Yr. $1,500/R $3,350/OS
State University of New York/College at New Paltz, New Paltz
Graphic Design
    B $1,564/R $3,414/OS
State University of New York/Erie Community College, Buffalo
Graphic Arts
    A/2-Yr.   '85/'86: $1,140/R $2,220/OD $3,300/OS
State University of New York/Fashion Institute of Technology, New
York
Advertising Communications, Advertising Design
    A,B $1,500/R $2,850/OS
State University of New York/Community College of the Fingerlakes,
Canandaigua
Graphic Arts
    A/2-Yr.   '85/'86: $1,334/R $2,558/OS
State University of New York/Mohawk Valley Community College,
Utica
Advertising, Design and Production
    A/2-Yr. $1,237/R $2,387/OS
State University of New York/Onondaga Community College, Syracuse
Graphic Arts and Advertising
    A/2-Yr.   *$1,364/R   *$2,806/OD   *$4,200/OS
State University of New York/Rockland Community College, Suffern
Graphic Arts
    A/2-Yr.   *$1,176/R   *$2,296/OS
State University of New York/Ulster County Community College,
Stone Ridge
Advertising Design and Graphic Technology
    C/2-Yr.   '85/'86: $1,472/R $4,172/OS
Syracuse University, Syracuse
Advertising Art and Design, Graphic Arts
    B $8,390

Villa Maria College of Buffalo, Buffalo
Graphic Communications Technology
C,A/2-Yr. *$3,770
NORTH CAROLINA
Anson Technical College, Ansonville
Commercial Art
A/2-Yr. $168/R $780/OS
Atlantic Christian College, Wilson
Graphics
B $4,300
Central Piedmont Community College, Charlotte
Commercial Art, Advertising Design, Interior Design, Graphic Arts
Management, Printing
A/2-Yr. $159/R $771/OS
Fayetteville Technical Institute, Fayetteville
Commercial Art and Advertising Design
C,A/2-Yr. $171/R $783/OS
Forsyth Technical Institute, Winston-Salem
Graphic Arts
C $168/R $780/OS
Guilford Technical Community College, Jamestown
Advertising and Commercial Art
A/2-Yr. $186/R $798/OS
James Sprunt Technical College, Kenansville
Commercial Art
A $177/R $789/OS
Pitt Community College, Greenville
Commercial Art, Graphic Design
A/2-Yr. $171/R $783/OS
Southwestern Technical College, Sylva
Commercial Art and Advertising
A $165/R $777/OS
Technical College of Alamance, Haw River
Commercial Art and Advertising
A $162/R $774/OS
Winsalm College, Winston-Salem
Commercial Art
C,A/2-Yr. '84/'85: $2,560
NORTH DAKOTA
Bismarck Junior College, Bismarck
Commercial Art
A/2-Yr. $1,138/R $2,206/OS
North Dakota State School of Science, Wahpeton
Graphic Arts
C/2-Yr. $1,038/R $2,106/OS

Valley City State College, Valley City
Graphics and Commercial Art
    A $1,128/R $2,196/OS
OHIO
Akron, University of, Akron
Commercial Art
    A $1,784/R $4,037/OS
Art Academy of Cincinnati, Cincinnati
Graphic Design
    B $4,370
Ashland College, Ashland
Commercial Art
    B   *$6,998
Cincinnati Technical College, Cincinnati
Graphic Communications Technology
    A/2-Yr. $1,650/R $2,640/OS
Cincinnati, University of, Cincinnati
Graphic Design
    B $2,091/R $4,989/OS
Clark Technical College, Springfield
Commercial Art
    A/2-Yr. $1,368/R $2,628/OS
Cleveland Institute of Art, Cleveland
Graphic Design
    B $6,250
Columbus College of Art and Design, Columbus
Commercial Art, Advertising Art and Design, Graphic Arts
    B $5,880
Columbus Technical Institute, Columbus
Graphic and Communication Arts
    A/2-Yr. $1,260/R $2,844/OS
Cuyahoga Community College/Western Campus, Parma
Graphic Communications Management and Technology
    A/2-Yr. $945/R $1,260/OD $2,520/OS
Lorain County Community College, Elyria
Graphics Design Technology
    A/2-Yr. $1,148/R $1,553/OD $3,263/OS
Ohio University, Athens
Graphic Design
    B $2,060/R $4,170/OS
Sinclair Community College, Dayton
Commercial Art, Graphic Arts Technology, Advertising
    A/2-Yr. $1,035/R $1,395/OD $1,712/OS
Terra Technical College, Fremont
Graphic Arts Communication

A $1,496/R $2,714/OS
Youngstown State University, Youngstown
Advertising and Public Relations, Advertising Art and Design,
Graphics Technology
B,A   '85/'86: $1,335/R $2,310/OS
OKLAHOMA
Northern Oklahoma College, Tonkawa
Graphic Arts Technology
C,A/2-Yr.   '85/'86: $431/R $1,246/OS
Oklahoma Christian College, Oklahoma City
Advertising Design
B   *$3,130
Oklahoma, University of, Norman
Advertising Art and Design
B,M   '85/'86: $866/R $2,523/OS
Oral Roberts University, Tulsa
Commercial Art
B $4,480
Rogers State College, Claremore
Graphic Arts
A/2-Yr.   '85/'86: $535/R $1,516/OS
Western Oklahoma State College, Altus
Commercial Art
A/2-Yr.   *$485/R   *$1,415/OS
OREGON
Clackamas Community College, Oregon City
Graphic Arts
C,A/2-Yr.   *$630/R   *$2,370/OS
Mount Hood Community College, Gresham
Graphic Design, Graphics Technology
A,C/2-Yr. $645/R $3,240/OS
Oregon State University, Corvallis
Graphic Arts
B   '85/'86: $1,449/R $4,152/OS
Portland Community College, Portland
Graphics Reproduction
A/2-Yr.   *675/R   *$1,425/OD   *$2,991/OS
PENNSYLVANIA
Beaver College—Glenside
Graphic Design
B $7,200
California University of Pennsylvania, California
Graphic Communications Technology
B   *$1,860/R   *$3,128/OS
Cedar Crest College, Allentown

Graphic Art
 B $7,610
Harrisburg Area Community College, Harrisburg
 Commercial Art
 A/2-Yr. *$918/R *$1,868/OD *$2,818/OS
Lackawanna Junior College, Scranton
 Graphic Arts
 A/2-Yr. $2,970
La Roche College, Portland
 Graphic Arts, Graphic Design
 B $4,760
Luzerne County Community College, Nanticoke
 Commercial Art
 C,A/2-Yr. $1,170/R $2,205/OD $3,240/OS
Montgomery County Community College, Blue Bell
 Commercial Art
 A/2-Yr. $1,074/R $2,094/OD $3,154/OS
Philadelphia College of Art, Philadelphia
 Graphic Design
 B '84/'85: $6,500
Saint Vincent College, Latrobe
 Graphic Design
 B $5,940
Williamsport Area Community College, Williamsport
 Advertising and Commercial Art, Graphic Arts
 A/2-Yr. $1,563/R $3,338/OD $5,112/OS
RHODE ISLAND
 Rhode Island School of Design, Providence
 Graphic Design
 B,M $9,635
SOUTH CAROLINA
 Chesterfield-Marlboro Technical College, Cheraw
 Graphics Technology
 A/2-Yr. $660/R $740/OD $1,040/OS
SOUTH DAKOTA
 Black Hills State College, Spearfish
 Commercial Art, Graphics
 A,B $1,794/R $2,904/OS
 Northern State College, Aberdeen
 Commercial Art
 A *$1,263/R *$2,306/OS
TENNESSEE
 Austin Peay State University, Clarksville
 Advertising and Commercial Art
 A *$1,143/R *$3,573/OS

Chattanooga State Technical Community College, Chattanooga
Advertising and Commercial Art
A/2-Yr.   *$639/R   *$3,069/OS
Memphis College of Art, Memphis
Advertising Art and Design
B $5,215
Nashville State Technical Institute, Nashville
Graphic Arts
C   *$639/R   *$3,069/OS
TEXAS
Amarillo College, Amarillo
Commercial Art
C,A/2-Yr.   *$353/R   *$600/OD   *$1,560/OS
Central Texas College, Killeen
Commercial Art
A/2-Yr. $256/R $690/OS
East Texas State University, Commerce
Advertising Art and Design
B $870/R $3,990/OS
Lamar University, Beaumont
Commercial Art
B $880/R $4,000/OS
Lee College, Baytown
Graphic Arts
C,A/2-Yr. $294/R $594/OD $1,314/OS
Navarro College, Corsicana
Commercial Art
A/2-Yr. $712/R $832/OD $868/OS
North Texas State University, Denton
Advertising Art
B,M $882/R $4002/OS
Sam Houston State University, Huntsville
Advertising and Graphic Design
B $880/R $4,000/OS
San Antonio College, San Antonio
Advertising Art and Design
A/2-Yr.   *$226/R   *$308/OD   *$574/OS
San Jacinto College North, Houston
Graphic Design
A/2-Yr. $330/R $630/OD $1,290/OS
Southwest Texas State University, San Marcos
Commercial Art
B   *$902/R   *$4,022
Texas State Technical Institute/Waco Campus, Waco
Commercial Art and Advertising

A $534/R $3,774/OS
Texas Tech University, Lubbock
Advertising Art and Design
B $862/R $3,982/OS
Texas Woman's University, Denton
Advertising Art and Design
B,M $882/R $4,002/OS
Tyler Junior College, Tyler
Graphics Communication Technology
A/2-Yr. $260/R $560/OD $1,070/OS
UTAH
Brigham Young University, Provo
Graphic Arts Technology, Graphic Design
A,B $1,550
Dixie College, Saint George
Graphic Arts
C,A/2-Yr. $809/R $2,109/OS
Snow College, Ephraim
Commercial Art
A/2-Yr. $813/R $2,115/OS
Utah Technical College, Provo
Commercial Art, Graphics
C,A $936/R $2,493/OS
Utah Technical College, Salt Lake City
Commercial Art
A $975/R $2,664/OS
VIRGINIA
Central Virginia Community College, Lynchburg
Commercial Art
A/2-Yr. $610/R $3,490/OS
Marymount College of Virginia, Arlington
Commercial Art
A,B $6,150
Norfolk State College, Norfolk
Graphic Design
B   '85/'86: $1,200/R $2,140/OS
Northern Virginia Community College, Annandale
Commercial Art
A/2-Yr. $765/R $3,645/OS
Thomas Nelson Community College, Hampton
Commercial Art
A/2-Yr. $771/R $3,651/OS
Tidewater Community College/Frederick Campus, Portsmouth
Graphic Arts
A/2-Yr. $765/R $3,645/OS

Virginia Intermont College, Bristol
Graphic Arts
   B $4,375
Virginia Western Community College, Roanoke
Commercial Art
   A/2-Yr. $850/R $3,730/OS
WASHINGTON
Centralia Community College, Centralia
Commercial Art
   A/2-Yr. $699/R $2,754/OS
Central Washington University, Ellensburg
Graphic Design
   B $1,212/R $4,206/OS
Highline Community College, Midway
Advertising Design/Illustration
   A/2-Yr. $699/R $2,754/OS
Seattle Central Community College, Seattle
Advertising Art and Design, Graphic Arts Technology
   C,A/2-Yr. $699/R $2,754/OS
Spokane Falls Community College, Spokane
Advertising Art
   A/2-Yr. $711/R $2,766/OS
Walla Walla College, College Place
Graphics Technology
   B $6,445
Washington, University of, Seattle
Graphic Design
   B $1,590/R $4,446/OS
WEST VIRGINIA
Concord College, Athens
Commercial Art, Advertising
   B $908/R $2,418/OS
Shepherd College, Shepherdstown
Commercial Art
   A,B $890/R $2,400/OS
West Liberty State College, West Liberty
Commercial Art
   B $900/R $2,410/OS
WISCONSIN
Lakeshore Technical Institute, Cleveland
Graphic Arts
   C $900/R $2,391/OD $6,306/OS
Madison Area Technical College, Madison
Commercial Art
   A/2-Yr. $738/R $2,229/OD $6,114/OS

Milwaukee Area Technical College, Milwaukee
  Commercial Art
  A/2-Yr.   No tuition information available
Silver Lake College, Manitowoc
  Commercial Art
  A $4,600
Western Wisconsin Technical Institute, La Crosse
  Commercial Art
  A/2-Yr. $900/R $2,391/OD $6,306/OS
Wisconsin, University of, Milwaukee
  Graphics
  B,M   '85/'86: $1,448/R $4,516/OS
Wisconsin, University of, Oshkosh
  Commercial Art
  B   '85/'86: $1,267/R $3,900/OS
WYOMING
Northwest Community College, Powell
  Commercial Art and Offset Production
  C,A/2-Yr. $570/R $1,410/OS

Chapter III

Tools of the Trade

Listed below are most of the "tools" you might find in an art department. The items marked with an asterisk (*) should be purchased if you intend to begin free-lancing. This listing covers the essential needs of an artist doing design, layout, and pasteup. Materials for a specialty, such as illustration, are not necessarily included. In many cases brand names are used. This in no way implies any superiority of a particular product—just personal preference or familiarity.

Drawing Board or Table: An adjustable one (for height and tilt of work surface) is preferable. It is possible, however, to keep a free-lancer's initial investment down by buying a legless board that can be placed on any table available. Art supply stores carry these boards. Some have a "true" edge (metal) on one or both sides for use with a T-square; others have a parallel bar that slides up and down on a metal cable. I suggest an approximate *minimum* size of 3' (width) by 2' (depth)

Drawing Board Covering: Plasticized and rubberized materials are sold, by the foot, to protect the wood working surface. Double-backed masking tape placed around the perimeter of the board will secure the covering material. To minimize the cost to a free-lancer, a large sheet of lightweight cardboard, cut to fit, would suffice.

Lighting: Unless set up with excellent overhead lighting or natural window light, it is advisable for the board to have its own light source (usually clamped on). Lamps are available that take a fluorescent tube or a 60- to 100-watt bulb. Both have a flexible arm, enabling you to pull the light directly over your work when

Drawingboard with light, parallel bar, and tape dispenser. Items displayed are: (top row, left to right) circle template, proportional scale, pen set, india (black) ink, revolving tray; (bottom row, left to right) triangle, work in progress, X-acto knife, pen, pica pole, jar of One Coat (adhesive).

desired. My preference is for fluorescent lighting, which cuts down glare and eliminates shadows on the work.

Stock: Each art department has its own preferences in the materials used for doing roughs, pasteups, and so on. In general, you need a supply of white, smooth-surfaced cardboardlike material on which to paste down your type or other components of the job. I specify smooth in case it is necessary to draw lines in ink, in addition to pasting type in position. Illustration board is sold in all art supply stores, but it is relatively expensive and for the most part not necessary. Ask the salesperson for 10-point (approximately) plate bristol or equivalent. Large sheets are more cost-effective than material sold in pads if you don't mind having to cut the sheet into pieces of workable size. A lightweight tissue paper is advisable, though not an absolute necessity, for covering a finished pasteup. It protects the work, shows your professionalism, and gives the client a place to note corrections without marking on the work itself. You also need paper on which to do roughs when required. This paper, sold in pads, is called a "layout" or "visualizer" pad. Buy the one with the largest sheet size so that you can do larger-sized roughs without having to tape several small sheets together.

Adhesives and Solvents: You need some method to attach the type and other components to the bristol board. Many agency and printing plant art departments use wax applied with a waxing machine (either a large, centralized machine or a hand-held one). Waxing is a very clean adhesive method, but it causes problems when pasteups are transported in weather that is either bitter cold or extremely hot. Rubber cement, either in a jar with brush or in a spray can, is popular. I do not advise the spray can for three reasons: 1) it is more expensive than other methods; 2) overspray is difficult to control; 3) you run the risk of inhalation. Rubber cement can be bought in cans or jars of various sizes. (Usually the smallest sizes come equipped with a brush. A secure bond with rubber cement is achieved by coating two surfaces: the type or other component that is to be pasted down and the board on which it is to be pasted. A product called One Coat, which is similar in consistency to rubber cement, requires coating only the item to be pasted down and allowing it to dry. This product speeds production time, but I have not seen it for sale in small containers. A thinner (solvent) for rubber cement and One Coat is available in several sizes. It is needed for thinning the cement when it becomes too thick to apply easily. It is also used for removing type or other components from the board when necessary (with a metal squirt can designed for the purpose).

Measuring Devices: Work that is to be printed is measured and discussed in *picas*. Therefore, you need a ruler at least twelve inches long marked in picas (sometimes called a *pica pole* or a *pica scale*). An eighteen- or twenty-four-inch pica ruler is even more desirable. Manufacturers often print other measurements—

either agate or inches—on the back of the pica ruler. If you can find the latter, it should be all you need in the way of a measuring device.

Cutting Tools: The most commonly used tool for cutting out type and other components is the X-acto knife, a long, thin handle that screws open to accept a small, sharp blade. X-acto blades are numbered, with #11 and #16 being my favorites. The thinness of the blade allows cutting between lines of type with more precision than with scissors. Scissors, also, may get gummed up from the adhesive on the back of the type or other component; when the knife blade has dulled or picked up too much adhesive, it can easily be changed. A mat-knife makes it easier to cut through heavy cardboard materials, but it is not an absolute necessity. You can make several passes in the same track with your X-acto knife and achieve the same results.

Horizontal and Vertical Alignment/Ruling Equipment: The horizontal devices are the T-square and the parallel bar. A T-square that is just short of the width of your drawing board will be less expensive than a parallel bar. The drawback of the T-square, unless there is a track or guide for it to slide on, is that you must constantly use one hand to keep the top of the "T" tight against the side of the board. Failure to do this will cause your work to be crooked. The parallel bar, running on its own cable, assures horizontal alignment (unless the cable stretches too much or breaks).

Vertical alignment/ruling is handled with triangles of varying sizes. One side will always be perpendicular to your T-square or parallel bar; the other side will be at an angle: 30, 45, or 60 degrees, depending on the triangle you choose. If at first you have no job that calls for alignment of any specified angle, it matters little which one you choose. Art departments usually have a large assortment of triangles, but a beginning free-lancer can get by with just one—as large as possible. The drafting machine is designed to provide both horizontal and vertical alignment in one piece of equipment, it is not widely used in agency or printer art departments, and it is fairly expensive.

Pens: Art departments have a variety of pens for different purposes: hand-lettering specialists need Speedball or calligraphy pens; artists who do any amount or ruling require technical pens; illustrators may prefer to draw with ultra-fine-point felt-tip pens. Other felt-tip pens called markers can be used for executing roughs. They are sold in every color imaginable and in several nib sizes, from fine-point to chisel-point. Unless you anticipate doing a lot of hand lettering, it is not necessary to spend money for Speedball or calligraphy pens. Technical pens can be purchased individually or in sets; purchasing one would be a good start. They are ordered by the thickness of line desired, from thinnest to widest, as follows: 000, 00, 0, 1, 2, 3, etc. The 0 or 00 gives the most versatility. Markers are not as easy for a beginner to handle as colored pencils for doing roughs; better skip the purchase of markers at first.

Pencils: Pencils come in an almost endless array of colors, thicknesses, and hardness of lead: each has its special purpose. A minimum requirement for a beginning free-lancer would be several non-repro (reproducible) blue pencils, a few medium-soft lead pencils (#2B or #3B is fine), and a starting set of colored pencils (Prismacolor pencils and other brands can be bought individually as well as in sets).

Erasers: Erasers also come in a variety of colors and uses: general-purpose rubber eraser for eliminating pencil marks (soft, pliable, often pink); ink eraser for stubborn ink marks (hard, very abrasive, usually white); kneaded eraser for pencil, pastel, and charcoal (usually gray, can be shaped to any convenient form; art gum eraser for removal of pencil marks from inked art (greaseless, crumbles with use, yellowish-white); rubber-cement pickup to remove excess cement from pasteups (hard, off-white); electric eraser for general use (nibs are interchangeable; can be soft or abrasive. As a free-lancer, you definitely need rubber-cement pickup and an art gum or a general-purpose eraser. The ink eraser might be useful, but other ways of eliminating ink marks are better and will be discussed later.

Tape: Work is fastened to a drawing board with metal pins or tape. Masking tape is available with adhesive on one side only or on both sides, called double-backed. It is sold in several widths: ¼", ½", ¾", 1", etc. Cellophane tape may be clear, frosted, white, or red. The white and red tapes have special uses in pasteup, which is discussed in the following paragraph. Specialty preprinted tapes may be used for borders or in place of ruled ink lines. A roll of ½″ masking tape adhesive one side and a roll of ½″ double-backed should get the beginning free-lancer started. The other tapes, though useful, can be dispensed with initially.

Opaquing materials: Both the white and red cellophane tapes are used as opaquing devices and can take the place of a white tempera paint or a black india ink (both used with a brush). But most often the tapes are used in *conjunction* with the white tempera (or other "white-out" product) and black ink. The size of the area to be opaqued determines which material to use. As the white and red tapes are reasonably expensive, an initial investment can be reduced by purhasing only the white tempera, a good black ink and a small (⅛″ or less diameter) sable or camel's-hair brush.

Proportional Scale: Because it is round, it is often called a "wheel." Easy to use, it lets an artist figure the percentage of reduction or enlargement needed for any component of the job. The percentage information is marked on or attached to the component and given to the cameraperson. A free-lancer definitely should have a wheel.

Overlay/window materials: When a piece is to be printed in more than one color and the colors will touch each other, it is necessary to separate them for the printer. This is done by attaching overlays (one for each color) using amberlith (orange in color) or rubylith (red in color). The overlay is opaque to a camera, but the artist can see through to the work underneath. The film, which is gelatinous with a plasticized backing, cuts easily with a knife. The area to be in color remains red or orange; the rest is peeled away. Other uses such as "knockouts" are explained in the next chapter. Clear and frosted acetates are also used for overlays: Type and other components are often pasted onto clear acetate: frosted acetate is most commonly used for ink work. Parapaque and Formopaque are dark red sticky-back materials that can be cut and peeled from wax paper backings. They are primarily used for "windows," a term that is defined in the next chapter. You need not purchase any of the above materials to begin free-lancing. When needed, however, amberlith, rubylith, and acetate can be purchased in pad form, in varying sheet sizes. Parapaque and Formopaque can be bought by the single sheet.

Templates: Making circles, ovals (ellipses), boxes, and other shapes is simple with the right template. The most common templates are made of a rigid plastic and are often green. Numerous in art departments, they are not vital for the beginner's shopping list.

Preprinted lettering, lines, and shapes: Art departments usually have a large inventory of this material. It comes in two forms: that which is rubbed on with a dull pencil, and that which has a sticky back and is cut out with a knife. I recommend the cutout type (Formatt, for one) for the beginner for several reasons: the rub-on is a little touchier to work with; it should be sprayed, for protection, with a fixative when finished; and it must be scraped off the work surface when a mistake is made. The cutout variety, if placed very lightly, can be repositioned indefinitely and needs no protection. Available are alphabets in several hundred type styles, lines in many widths, assorted shapes in varying sizes, fancy borders, and pages of intricate designs. A free-lancer will probably acquire his/her own inventory over a period of time, buying only when the need arises. Many art supply stores carry a particular manufacturer's preprinted type. A catalog of the styles available is usually for sale at a reasonable price—sometimes, but not often, free! Becoming familiar with the typefaces in any manufacturer's catalog will help the beginning artist, so I advise getting one, whatever the cost.

Light Table: Most art departments have some method of backlighting a piece of work so that it can be traced onto another paper or lightweight cardboard or for preparing intricate overlays. Sophisticated light tables are freestanding units with legs, well-diffused lighting, true sides for use with a T-square, and frosted glass set into a metal frame. Many "homemade" varieties are nothing more than a wooden box with one or two fluorescent tubes inside and frosted glass inset, or secured with tape, on top. If you're a beginning free-lancer and need to trace something, any sunlit window in your home will do. If working vertically is a problem, however, a piece of frosted glass and a small, unshaded lamp will suffice: Sit in a chair, feet flat on the floor; place one edge of the glass on your knees and the other edge on any piece of furniture approximately knee-high; and place the lamp on the floor as close as possible to the center of the glass.

Clip art: The most convenient way for an art department to have access to reproducible illustration, without employing an illustrator, is to buy clip art (not a brand name). This monthly service is less popular with agencies than with newspaper and printer art departments. The illustrations are generic in nature, so the services of an illustrator would still be necessary for some specific drawing. Though the fee for the service might be considered reasonable, unless a free-lancer needed enormous amounts of camera-ready illustration, it would not be a wise investment.

Airbrush Equipment: This specialized equipment is found in many, but certainly not all, art departments. Working with an airbrush requires particular training that not every artist has had. Inks or paints are sprayed through a nozzle under the pressure from a tank of carbon dioxide (CO_2). Art departments that do custom illustration or a large amount of photo retouching would most likely have airbrush equipment and at least one artist proficient in its use.

Chapter IV

Glossary of Terms

A glossary of terms would be just a technical vocabulary to memorize unless the terms are understood in context as well. So...

We'll start our usage of these strange new words by inventing an agency, clients, and the work that they need performed. The glossary of terms follows the scenario.

Mr. and Mrs. Newfolk are seated at the conference table at the ABC Agency. Their new business, FanciWoods, Inc., manufactures an assortment of wood decorator items. They need *camera-ready* art for a *logo*, business cards, a self-mailer with tear-off reply card, and a catalog with pictures of their products.

ABC Agency promises that several *thumbnail* ideas for the logo will be ready by the end of the week. After the logo design is chosen, the agency will use this important *component* on the *rough layout* for the self-mailer and the twenty-four-page catalog. Mrs. Newfolk is concerned about the front and back covers of the catalog and asks to see a *comprehensive layout* for those two pages only. She shows the *account executive* and the art director a large, horizontal color print of their new building. Everyone agrees that if they *crop* a little sky and foreground, the photo would be an attractive front and back cover *wraparound*. As the covers will be a *four-color-process* printing job, *color separations* and *color keys* will be needed for the comprehensive. Placement of the logo will be important: either as an *overprint* in the sky area, or as a *reverse* out of the green grass in the foreground. The Newfolks are sure that the reverse would be more effective. It is also decided that the covers will *bleed* on all four sides.

The black-and-white *continuous-tone* photographs of their products are spread out on the table. Twelve of the best photos will be printed as *halftones* in the *guts* of the catalog.

The size of the self-mailer is discussed next, as well as how it will fold. *French fold, gate fold* and *Z fold* are not options for this piece. But a *double-parallel fold* for a *legal-size* mailer or a *letterfold* for a *letter-size* mailer will work. The Newfolks prefer the latter, with one *perf* and one *score* to accomplish the folding. With this information, ABC Agency can now start work. An appointment is made with the Newfolks to see the logo thumbnails on Friday.

An artist begins work immediately on the logo. She feels strongly that she should use a *serif* typeface for the company name. She selects two *italic* and three *roman* serif typefaces to work with. Incorporated into her design are the company's address and phone line in a compatible *sans-serif* type. She indicates this information *flush right* on one thumbnail, *flush left* on three others, and *centered* on the last. When the Newfolks arrive to see the thumbnail sketches, they instantly choose the *boldface* typestyle that has been shaded to simulate a 40 percent *screen*. The screen will be used unless the logo appears reversed, as on the catalog cover. The artist can now do the *mechanical* on the logo and shoot the *PMT*s necessary to board the business card *four-up* to shorten the printer's *pressrun*. Another appointment is scheduled for the Newfolks to see camera-ready art on the business card, the remaining roughs, and the comprehensive catalog cover.

Two weeks later, the Newfolks approve the roughs and are delighted with the catalog cover and the business card. *Stock* and *ink* samples are shown and decided upon. They have brought in the final *copy* for the self-mailer and the catalog, including the *indicia* for the reply card. Although the roughs indicate the copy to be typeset *ragged-right*, the Newfolks would be happier with it set *justified*. They want the name of the item to be larger than the description and price. The art director assures them that the name will be at least one *point* larger, perhaps in boldface for extra emphasis. He will *spec* the type for the typesetter and is confident that with a 30-*pica* column width the description will be no less than 10-point type with a two-point *lead*. With the addition of a little more *air* between paragraphs, the copy will be very readable. The Newfolks are satisfied but want to *proof* the *galleys* for *typos* before they are pasted up.

While the copy is being typeset, boards are prepared for the self-mailer and the catalog. After checking with the printer, a *folding dummy* is made. The catalog will be printed four pages up, with three eight-page *signatures* to *collate*, trim, and *saddle stitch*. The artist can board the work in two-page *printer flats* or four-page printer flats. Her board will accommodate four pages at a time, but she dislikes pasting up pages *head-to-head*. More attention must be given to having the *pagination* right, also. She opts to do her pasteup just two pages at a time.

Carefully, she rules out the page size boundaries in *non-repro blue* pencil on the *base art*. The maxium *image area* is also drawn lightly in blue, allowing for the *gripper* requirements of the press. The *crop marks* and fold and perf lines are indicated in ink. Acetate and amberlith *overlays* are attached where needed and *registered* to the base art. None of the photographs will need a *knockout*, but the Newfolks would like a thin ruled line around each photo. The artist determines the reduction or enlargement necessary on each so that they will all print exactly the same size. She rules the photo borders on the base art and cuts windows on amberlith overlays.

The proofed and corrected galleys arrive and the type is pasted in position. All that remains is final approval by the Newfolks before the work is printed.

Following are definitions of the terms set in italics in the foregoing scenario:

account executive (AE)   The person in an agency who works most closely with the client.
air   White space that will not be printed. White space is often considered one component or design element of a piece.
base art   The mechanical that is taped directly to the drawing board and contains most of the pasted-up components.

bleed   Printing that goes all the way to the edge of one or more sides of the paper.

boldface   Type that is heavier and thicker than the more commonly used "medium" or "regular" type. Boldface is used in headlines or for emphasis.

camera-ready   Finished art, ready to go to the printer.

centered   Having all components aligned one beneath the other so that all center points form a straight vertical line.

collate   To assemble in order for binding. In the Newfolks' twenty-four-page brochure, the printer decides to use three eight-page signatures. They are placed inside each other, rather than on top of each other. After printing, the signatures must be put in the proper order inside each other, or collated, before being trimmed and bound.

color key   Filmlike material in each of the four colors that is exposed, with light, to its corresponding negative, producing a positive. The four colored positives are placed in proper alignment (*see* registration) on top of each other to produce a facsimile of the original full-color artwork. The color key is used to check the color against the original and show the client how the printed version will look.

color separation   Electronic or laser equipment that "reads" the amount of each of the four colors in the piece that is to be duplicated, separating them from each other. A negative, consisting of dot groupings in varying densities, is made for each of the four colors to be printed.

component   Single part or piece of a job. For example, the logo, the main headline, and a photo would each be one component of a whole job.

comprehensive layout   Extremely detailed work, looking as much as possible like the printed piece. Type is often set to accomplish this purpose.

continuous-tone   Photograph from which a halftone is made; *see* halftone.

copy (also called text)   The words that comprise one component of a piece of work and carry the client's message.

crop   To eliminate unwanted portions of a photograph, painting, or drawing.

crop marks   Small lines, usually in ink, placed on all four corners of the mechanical to indicate the exact size of the piece of work. When the press sheet is larger than called for by the finished work, the crop marks give the cutter instructions as to where to trim. Fold marks and perf marks are also placed on the mechanical to give instructions for those functions.

flush left   Having all components lined up so that the left sides form a straight vertical line.

flush right   Having all components lined up so that the right sides form a straight vertical line.

folding dummy   Blank paper, not necessarily the same size as the job to be printed, which is folded where it will fold when printed. Multipage work requires signatures.

four-color-process   Printing that is done in four specific colors: yellow, magenta (red), cyan (blue), and black. Using these four colors in combination with each other and in varying strengths, every other color can be reproduced. Used mainly to print original full-color paintings or drawings and colored photographs (either print or slide).

four-up (also two-up, eight-up, six-up, etc.)   The same piece of work placed on the mechanical multiple times. When the work to be printed is small in size and the number to be printed is large, an artist may be asked to prepare it in "ups," thus shortening the printer's pressrun.

French fold, gate fold, Z fold, double parallel fold, letter fold. These are best described graphically. *See* illustrations.

galleys   All the typeset copy for a given job, in one or more continuous sheets of typesetting film, before it has been cut apart for pasteup.

gripper   On most smaller presses, allowance made for the place where the printing plate attaches to the press. Although the printing plate is 11″ × 17″ and the work to be printed is the same size, a portion of the 17″ will not print because the press is gripping the plate along that side. The image area, therefore, must be smaller than 17″.

guts   The inside pages of a piece of work having at least eight pages. Four pages comprise the covers; all other pages are the guts.

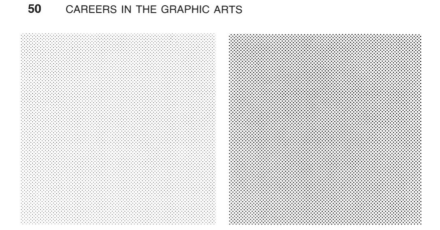

Left: 10% screen; right, 30% screen.

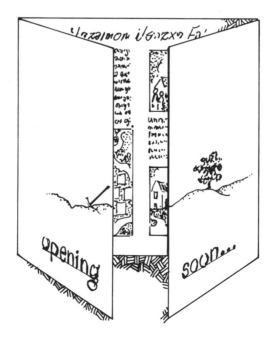

Gate fold.

Z fold.

Reverse.

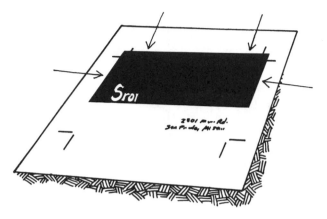

Bleed.

Double parallel fold.

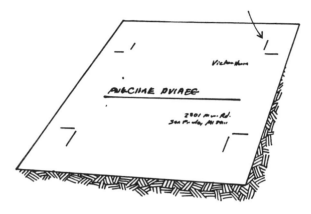

Crop marks.

French fold.

halftones   Photoengraving of a photograph, converting it into a pattern of dots, dense where the continuous-tone photo was darkest and sparse in the lighter areas. *See* screen.

head-to-head   On a four-page flat, arrangement of pages with tops together so that two are right side up and two are upside down to the artist.

image area   Area on any piece of work that will be inked and printed.

indicia   The information that must appear on a mailing piece. Postal regulations require very specific formats for reply cards and other mailing pieces that advertisers use frequently.

ink   The colored fluid that is used to print on stock.

italic   Type that slants, usually to the right, so that it is not perpendicular to its baseline.

justified   Lines of type set flush with one another on the right as well as on the left.

knockout   Method of eliminating unwanted parts of a photograph when making a halftone. An amberlith (or rubylith) overlay is placed on the photo, and the background is "knocked out" by leaving overlay on the subject and peeling away the rest.

lead (leading)   The space, usually measured in points, between the baseline of one line of type and the baseline of the next line *minus* the point size of the type used. Type set 10/12 is 10-point type with two points of space, or lead.

legal-size   Paper that measures 8½″ × 14″.

letter-size   Paper that measures 8 ½″ × 11″.

logo   Company trademark, usually custom designed and consisting of the company name and/or a meaningful graphic symbol.

mechanical   Whether completed or in progress, the paper or lightweight board that has type pasted up, overlays attached, and is or will be camera-ready art; sometimes simply called artwork or pasteup.

non-repro blue   Special blue that is not reproduced by the camera. Marks made with a pencil or felt-tip pen in this color will not appear on the negative, so need not be erased.

overlay   Piece of artwork laid over and attached to the base art. When all the components cannot be applied to the base art, overlays are used to separate them.

overprint   Type or any other component that will print on or over another component such as a photo or painting.

pagination   Proper sequence of page numbers.

perf (perforation)   Straight line made up of dashes that puncture, rather than print, the paper. Performed on the press, perfing makes it possible for a portion of the printed piece to be torn off easily.

pica   Unit of typographical measurement. There are twelve points to one pica; six picas to one inch. The width of a column of type is expressed in picas.

point   Unit of measurement for type. There are 72 points to an inch. Type is identified by its point size, giving the height of the letter; e.g., 6-point type, 12-point type, 48-point type.

PMT (photomechanical transfer), also called photostat, or stat   The camera photographs the drawing or type that is needed for pasteup, exposing it to a piece of negative paper (rather than film). A positive piece of paper (receiver) of the same size is placed on top, and they are run together through a developing solution. The negative paper is discarded, and the positive is used for pasteup. PMTs are used when the original is too large or small for pasteup or must be returned to the client.

pressrun   Usually the number of sheets, rather than pieces, that are to be printed. The Newfolks are ordering 2,000 business cards. When the artist boards them four-up, the printer has to run only 500 sheets to obtain 2,000 cards. He has a pressrun of 500.

printer flats   The mechanicals of a multipage job. Printer flats can be two pages or more, depending on the size of the artist's drawing board. A twenty-four-page brochure, pasted up in two-page printer flats would have pages 1 and 24 on the same mechanical, pages 2 and 23, pages 3 and 22, etc.

proof (proofread)   To read typeset copy against the original, checking for errors.

ragged-right   Type or other components that are presented flush left and the right sides have no particular lineup.

register   Correct alignment of overlays to base art. Marks are placed on the base art, beyond the crop marks (if space permits), and each overlay receives identical marks that line up with, or register to, the marks on the base art. The marks most commonly used are circles with cross hairs, called registration marks.

reverse   The exact shape of a component, whether it is type or a logo, appearing as blank space. The shape of the component is formed by the printed portion of the paper surrounding its contours. The color of the paper showing through the unprinted space becomes the color of the component.

roman   Type that is straight up and down, perpendicular to its baseline.

rough layout   Similar to a thumbnail in its lack of detail, but usually prepared in the final size that will be printed. The components are laid out in the approximate position they will be when the work is ready to paste up. Rough layouts can be executed in lead pencil or in color with colored pencils or markers.

saddle stitch   One of many ways to bind a booklet or brochure. Two or three staples are placed vertically down the fold line of the pages.

sans serif   Type without serifs (*sans* is the French word for "without").

score   Deep groove along the fold line that compresses heavy paper or board. Without scoring, the paper or board would wrinkle or crack when folded.

screen (also called tint, especially when color is used)   Preprinted acetatelike material that consists of dots. Screens vary according to the density of dots (how many in one square inch) and are identified in percentages: 10% screen, 20% screen, 50% screen. When printing color, use of a screen lightens that color. Black can achieve many shades of gray, depending on the screen chosen. Red can become pink when printed with a 10% screen. Dark blue can become medium or light blue with the use of the proper screen. Screens enable the designer to add what appears to be another color to the job without actually doing so.

serif   Fine line projecting from a main stroke of a letter.

signature   Folded sheet that is one unit of a book. For an eight-page signature, for example, a sheet of paper is folded in quarters so that it forms a small book of eight pages with the tops of the pages uncut. The pages are then numbered in sequence (*see* pagination). When the paper is opened again, it provides a guide as to which pages will be together. The printer prints together the four pages that are shown on one side of the signature, then the four pages on the other side.

spec   To write specifications for typeset copy: typeface, point size, etc.

stock   The paper or other material that is to be printed.

thumbnail   Small (perhaps 3″ square), quick graphic interpretation of an idea without fine detail.

typo (typographical error)   Error found either in the original or the typeset copy.

window   Clear space that appears on a negative wherever opaque material has been placed on the mechanical. In a knockout the entire area of the subject (with no background) will appear as a window in the negative. Windows are rectangular or square when a photo is to be printed with background intact.

wraparound   In the Newfolks' case, a photo that does not stop at the expected place (the fold separating front and back covers), but continues. Type that departs from the normal column format and follows the contour of a photo or drawing is also called a wraparound.

Part 2

Chapter **V**

Elements of Design/Layout

Let's pretend, for Part 2, that you have your first job as a graphic artist either as free-lancer or employed by an agency. You have two assignments to work on immediately. First, Mrs. Jones and her partner, Mrs. Smith, have just opened a retail store that sells ladies' apparel, jewelry, and accessories. The name of the store is Rainbo-tique. They need a logo design, which will then be used on business cards, letterheads, and envelopes. Second, Mr. Green's company, Protektite, Inc., manufactures and installs burglar alarm systems for homes and businesses. Mr. Green also requires a logo design, business cards, letterheads, and envelopes.

Both customers have told you that they'd like to look at a minimum of three logo thumbnails. When one of the thumbnail designs has been chosen, each customer wants to see and approve the final artwork (mechanical) before its incorporation into the layout of their business card, letterhead, and envelope.

The logo is a major element (component) in the total design/layout of every piece to be printed. Indeed, the arrangement of the other elements that make up the business card or letterhead is usually determined by the size, shape, and placement of the logo. For this reason, the logo design is normally chosen and completed first.

So—it's time to design a logo. Where do you begin? Just in case you've never paid much attention to logos and their construction, I'll tell you about a reference book that is practically at your fingertips this very moment and is jam-packed with logos. You don't have to buy this book, nor do you have to check it out of

Familiar logos.

the library—it's the Yellow Pages section of your city's phone directory!

Open the Yellow Pages to Automobile Dealers–New Cars and notice that most dealerships advertise with the logo of a particular make of car. Look first for the Lotus, Mazda, Nissan, Saab, Volvo, and Chrysler logos. Then, for comparison, study the Dodge, Volkswagen, Porsche, Jaguar, and Peugeot logos. Do you see any difference? The first group of cars have logos composed of type only. The second group uses a graphic device or symbol (a jaguar for Jaguar, a shield for Porsche) *and* type.

Check several other products in your directory and look for logos. You'll note that many are nicely done with type alone. The type is always distinctive and has been chosen to project an image—about the company itself or its product. (We'll examine how type can play this important role in the next chapter.) Graphic devices as part of a logo are sometimes chosen for esthetic purposes only, but more often there is a definite tie-in with the company's name or product. Just as Jaguar uses a picture of the animal, a Chinese restaruant called "The Golden Dragon" might have a dragon; a plumbing contractor's logo could sport a wrench or other commonly used tool of the trade.

The logos shown here are so well known that even from a distance and at a quick glance you would know the name of the company and the product or service that it sells.

Essentially, all companies are hoping for the same thing—that their logo will become well recognized, even on a very local level. Rainbo-tique and Protektite are now dependent on *your* creativity to devise a logo that projects the company's image or product and leaves a lasting impression.

Let's begin with Rainbo-tique. Mrs. Jones and Mrs. Smith, in their preliminary meeting with you, talked a little about how they had chosen the name. Both viewed their new enterprise as a "boutique" but didn't care for anything as mundane as "J & S Boutique." They both loved bright colors and planned to use them abundantly in the shop's decor. The clothing and accessories stocked would also be trendy and colorful.

With the word "rainbow" as part of the name, it's easy to think of at least one graphic device that can be used for the thumbnails. A full rainbow? A partial rainbow? Perhaps full rainbow for one, partial rainbow for a second, and type only for the third. Now that was easy, wasn't it?

The type to be used is the other consideration. At the risk of being labeled sexist, I'm going to say that type styles can be thought of as feminine, masculine, or neuter. In the chapter on Typography and Typesetting, you'll see how it is possible to attach a gender to something as inanimate as a bunch of letters.

Rainbo-tique is owned and operated by women who sell ladies' apparel. The clothes they stock are trendy and colorful, not pastel and fragile. Their logo type should reflect this business profile: feminine or neuter, rather than masculine; sturdy, rather than fragile or delicate.

Now let's go on, for a moment, to Protektite, Inc. Using the same considerations, what is your first inclination? Should the type be feminine, masculine, or neuter? Would you be looking for a typeface that is fragile or sturdy?

Please note that the adjectives I've used are *my* adjectives only. I doubt that they appear in any typestyle book as a description of the typeface shown. Here are a few more to consider: a type can be playful or conservative; ultramodern, traditional, or old-fashioned.

Protektite, Inc. manufactures burglar alarms. The product itself suggests security and reliability. Mr. Green, the owner, was conservatively dressed and was a very direct (almost brusque), no-nonsense businessman.

With what you know of the product and the company owner, you'll undoubtedly be looking for type that is masculine or neuter, sturdy, conservative, and fairly traditional.

Will you use a graphic device or not? The name Protektite doesn't immediately suggest an object that could be used. Burglar alarms generally make a sound. Depicting a radiating sound is a possibility, but check first to see if any other company selling a similar product has used the idea. The window tape installed as part of the alarm system might lend itself to an interesting graphic device. Just remember, it's not absolutely necessary to incorporate a graphic as part of the logo. If something you think of has been done to death or is just "too cute," better stick with type only. For Protektite, I'd try a thumbnail using the tape idea and prepare two using type only.

After you've decided on the typestyles and graphic devices to be used, you'll probably sketch your ideas quickly in pencil. Perhaps you'll do as many as ten or twelve very rough thumbnail approaches per logo. The hardest part comes in the elimination process: choosing the three for each company that you intend to refine. The amount of refinement for a thumbnail is based on what the customer expects and the way your employer normally works.

I've seen thumbnails so rough that they bore little resemblance to the finished piece and others so detailed that they appeared to have been printed. In general, I'd say that if the customer were so extremely creative and able to imagine what his/her logo would look like, the customer would be the artist—not you. Don't leave too much to the imagination. Clearly show the typeface that you're suggesting and finish the graphic in enough detail so that it is recognizable. If the finished logo will be printed in color, work in color.

A word of advice: Do your best work, but if the customer dislikes the one design that you felt was your most brilliant effort, don't let it bruise your ego. There's nothing personal involved, and be the customer right or wrong (in your opinion), the customer is *always* right. Now, let's see what the finished logos might look like:

Rainbo-tique

ProtekTite
I N C O R P O R A T E D

You're ready now to lay out (design) the business cards, letter-heads, and envelopes for both companies.

A standard business card measures 3½″ horizontally, 2″ vertically, not a great deal of space for all the information that must appear. First is the logo or company name or both and one or two address lines. The address lines may or may not include the phone number. When the phone number is more important than the address (customers order by telephone rather than visit the location), the number is usually larger and on a line by itself. A personalized business card carries a name and job title. Often there is a line that briefly describes the company's product or service. Protektite, Inc. has this additional line: "Burglar Alarm Systems for Home and Office."

A standard letterhead measures 8½″ horizontally, 11″ vertically and contains the same information as the business card, minus an individual name and title. Occasionally, however, a letterhead has a list of corporate officers and their titles or a list of branch locations.

A standard envelope (called a # 10) measures 9½″ horizontally, 4⅛″ vertically and accommodates the letterhead when it is letter-folded (approximately in thirds). Its information is usually confined to logo and/or company name and address lines.

There are no written rules and regulations for component placement on business cards, letterheads, and envelopes. The few printer requirements are discussed in the chapter on Pasteup.

There are, however, commonly used approaches. It's never a question of right or wrong, but whether or not the piece is well balanced. The components must work well together and complement each other.

Picture, for a moment, a scale in the shape of a T, with two trays that hang on either side of the crossbar. What happens if all the weight is put into one tray? Of course, the scale won't balance and looks lopsided.

The components of a business card, a letterhead, and an envelope all have "weight." Even the white space that is not printed, when taken in conjunction with other components, can be considered to have weight.

In the three pieces that are being done for each company, we have a logo and at least two address lines. Protektite has a separate line for description and one for phone number. How much weight does each carry? The logo, being the largest component, would get my vote for being the heaviest. If you put the logo by itself in one tray of the imaginary scale, what other components would you need to counterbalance it?

Let's look at the commonly used approaches to business card, letterhead, and envelope design/layout. We'll position the finished logo, completing the layout with ruled lines to suggest the placement of type. Watch for balance.

The top layout is probably the most popular for an envelope. All the components are neatly stacked under one another in the upper left corner. The bottom layout, called an *end presentation*, runs the logo and address lines across the left end of the envelope. This arrangement is a bit more informal and is not used quite as often.

Where is the balance, you're probably asking. If all the components are on the left side of the envelope, the layout looks lopsided. You're right, of course. But when someone receives the envelope, what does it look like? In the upper right corner there is a canceled stamp or meter stamp and a postmark. Slightly below

and to the right of center are three or four lines of name and address. Now how do things balance?

The top and bottom business card layouts (p. 68) are almost identical, but mirror images. The logo has been placed to the left on one, to the right on the other. The rest of the components have been placed for a balanced appearance.

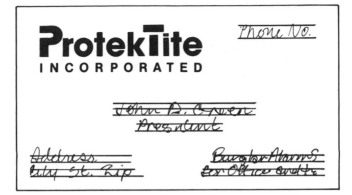

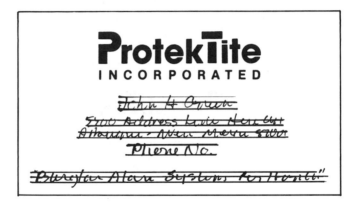

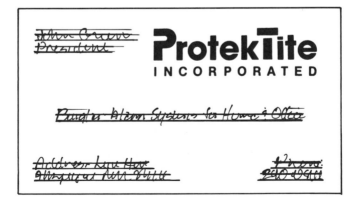

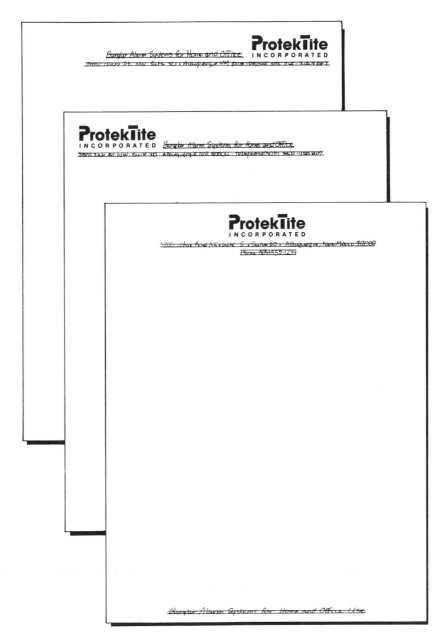

The middle card starts with a centered logo and places components in the space remaining below. The top two letterheads (p. 69) are mirror images, with the logo placed to the left or to the right. The bottom letterhead is the more formal, centered approach. The lines under the logo could be moved to the bottom of the letterhead to achieve even greater balance, but that arrangement is not seen as often.

Although the *specific* placement of components varies, the most commonly used layouts on business cards and letterheads are logo to the right, logo to the left, or logo centered. Envelopes must confine printing to the left side to make room for material added later.

Unfortunately, space permits us to work through the design/layout of only a few of the many pieces a graphic artist is called upon to do. Customers will want brochures, flyers, direct mailers, newspaper and Yellow Pages ads, invitations, announcements, posters, and more. You'll work with other components—paragraphs of typeset copy, photographs, and illustrations—as well as logos, address lines, and phone numbers.

The first step in the layout/design process is *thought*. Think about the company's product or service and the image the company wants to project. Think about your own impression of the company, gained from conversations with the owner or manager. Before your pencil ever touches a piece of paper, mental pictures should be coming into focus.

The physical organization and balance of the components on paper is second. It can be tedious and frustrating to keep switching lines around from left to right, top to bottom for that "just right" look. Take comfort in the fact that with experience it becomes possible to organize the whole layout, too, in your mind. This is a great timesaver when it happens. Alas, the customer cannot see what you "see," so you'll have to take the time to transfer it to paper.

What might be thought of as a last step in the design/layout process is criticism. Developing a critical eye is as important as developing any other creative ability. Criticism is healthy when it's creative and constructive. When you finish a piece, look at it as objectively as you can and ask yourself if it could be improved.

Sometimes the answer will be yes and, time permitting, you'll make the necessary adjustments.

Start examining the printed materials that are handed to you or come in the mail. Are they well organized? Well balanced? Does your eye travel from one component to the next in a logical, step-by-step manner?

Don't be intimidated by the fact that a particular piece was produced by a large and well-known advertising agency. Don't be afraid to be critical (in this case *you* are the potential customer). If the piece is disorganized, badly balanced, and difficult to read, think about how you might have handled it to make it better.

Chapter VI

Typesetting and Typography

When I first sat down to a typesetting machine, almost thirty years ago, it was a frustrating experience. The type I was setting was called *cold* type, to distinguish it from type that was cast from hot metal—quite naturally called *hot* type. The machine was slow and cranky, with no easy way to correct my many mistakes. The type, a strike-on type that used a carbon ribbon, was not perfect enough to take an enlargement. If I wanted larger type for the piece I was doing, I had to set it on another machine. Needless to say, jobs couldn't be completed quickly.

The computer age made cold typesetting a pleasure. Large computers with their interfacing developing units have given the industry phototypesetting. The letters are sharp enough to take substantial enlargement. Compare a phototypeset word with the same word that has been hand set, using a popular preprinted type (p. 74). Each word has been enlarged 300 percent. Do you see any difference with the naked eye? With a magnifying glass?

Monitors (cathode ray tubes or CRTs) allow you to see what you're typing. Editing functions enable you to preview the typed copy and make corrections before it is *run out* (sent to the printing unit, then to the chemical developing unit).

Some models display on the screen the words or lines you have set in the typestyle, point size, and arrangement desired. There's not much guesswork—"what you see is what you get." A typesetter can easily follow an artist's layout with this equipment. Other models require the typesetter to visualize the finished copy; everything looks the same on the monitor, although the operator has told the computer to change the point size, typestyle, or

ART

Phototypeset word.

ART

Hand-set word.

arrangement. Not every good typist has the ability to visualize—which is why I maintain that the best typesetters are, or should be, artistic.

A minimum of keystrokes is required to tell the computer that the copy should be set ragged right, ragged left, centered, or justified. Machines that accept eight or more typestyles *on line* (inserted and able to be accessed), mixing serif, sans serif, roman, and italic, enable an operator to set copy for many pieces in one sitting. See the accompanying examples.

Computer technology is advancing rapidly. For some time computers and their software have had the capability of composing an entire page for a flyer or brochure right on the screen. The copy can be one, two, or three columns of type, placed in position

Our goal has always been to provide a creative professional service at competitive prices. We feel we
have succeeded in offering you the experience and
insight of a large advertising agency, but with all of
the personal attention which only a small art department can provide. We would appreciate a chance to

Our goal has always been to provide a creative professional service at competitive prices. We feel we have
succeeded in offering you the experience and insight
of a large advertising agency, but with all of the personal attention which only a small art department can
provide. We would appreciate a chance to bid on your

Our goal has always been to provide a creative professional service at competitive prices. We feel we have
succeeded in offering you the experience and in-
which only a small art department can provide. We
would appreciate a chance to bid on your next brochure, catalog or annual report. Call 842-9040 for an

Our goal has always been to provide a creative
professional service at competitive prices. We feel
we have succeeded in offering you the experience
but with all of the personal attention which only a
small art department can provide. We would
appreciate a chance to bid on your next brochure,

*(1) Ragged right, serif type; (2) ragged left, sans serif type; (3) justified copy; (4)
centered copy.*

without benefit of pasteup. Recently the computer age has brought
us "desktop publishing," with graphics packages that allow illustrations to be done right on the keyboard and inserted into the
copy where desired. At the moment, desktop publishing cannot
produce the quality printing of phototypesetting units, but that is
sure to be available before long.

Where does that leave a good design, layout, and pasteup

person (or an illustrator, for that matter)? Well, note that I said, "Computers are able to do this or that..." Who tells the computer what to do?

First of all, any computerized typesetting machine needs an operator who is, in addition to being an excellent typist, "artistic." A machine, after all, can only execute commands. The thought, judgment, and design still come from a real, live person. Never will there be a graphics package (software) that can incorporate all of the items an illustrator might be called on to draw and render.

Second, prices for equipment are prohibitive to a small agency or graphics department, and businesses that do nothing but typesetting find it almost impossible to have the "latest" equipment. By the time "the latest" is delivered and installed, an even more sophisticated model is on the market. For that reason machines in use today vary in make, model, and age. If it is functional and making money, it is not obsolete.

I see no reason to believe that computers will replace illustrators or good design, layout, and pasteup people in the near future.

Meanwhile, back to the assignment at hand—the finished envelope, business card, and letterhead for Rainbo-tique and Protektite. Once the layouts have been approved by the customer, final type can be set. More choices!

Unless the customer has a definite typestyle in mind (most don't), you, the design/layout person, are usually the one to choose. Not only the typestyle you specify, but information about the point size, leading, and pica width must be given to the typesetter. The term for this information-giving process is *speccing* (from specification).

Businesses that specialize in setting type provide a brochure or booklet showing the typefaces/styles (called *fonts*) that they have available. The number can range from a few dozen to several hundred. Most agencies and printer art departments buy type from more than one place, thereby increasing the variety of styles available to them.

Type suitable for a logo design or the bold headline on a flyer or brochure is probably not suitable for *body copy* (also called *text*—the smaller lines of type that make up most of the reading matter). Text copy can be roman or italic, serif or sans serif, but it shouldn't call attention to itself by being unusual in its letter formation. The letters shouldn't be too thick or too thin, which would distract the eye from reading the copy. Contrast that with logo design, where you *want* the type to be distinctive and call attention to itself.

Limiting the number of typestyles used on any one piece (I would advise a maximum of three) adds cohesion and avoids a busy, checkerboard look. Most typefaces are part of an extended "family." A piece using just one typeface in addition to the logo type can be made interesting by varying the point size and using several members of the same family. The illustration (p. 78) shows several members of the large Helios family.

Text type rarely exceeds 18 points and normally is between 5 points and 14 points. Each machine produces a certain range of point sizes. Before speccing the type to be sent to a particular typesetter, it is wise to know the capability of his/her machine. A few point sizes are illustrated (p. 78) for comparison.

Leading is the number of points between the baseline of one word or line and the baseline of the next. You need to be as adept at math as you are creative. For instance, you have a space on your layout that is only two inches deep (vertical measurement—in this case, there is no problem with width). The customer has submitted a twelve-line poem to fill the space and says, "Make the type as big as possible." What do you tell the typesetter? Well, I've dealt with typesetters who would do all the figuring for me if I were pressed for time, but typesetting is an expensive per-hour charge, and I paid dearly for being in that much of a hurry. So brush up on your math!

There are 72 points to an inch. Your space is two inches deep; therefore you have 144 points of space to work with. Dividing the 144 points by 12 (the number of lines), you come up with 12 again, meaning that the largest point size that can be used is 12 point. That doesn't allow for any leading between lines and is called *set solid*. With few exceptions, type that is set solid is hard to read; even one point of leading helps a lot. Since the customer requested type as large as possible, I would tell the typesetter to use 11 point type with 1 point leading—expressed as 11/12.

If no leading is undesirable, then could we say "the more the

Helios

Helios Italic

Helios Bold

Helios Light

Helios Condensed

Helios Bold Condensed

Helios Extra Bold Condensed

6pt-This is an example of six point type.

8pt-This is an example of eight point type.

10pt-This is an example of ten point type.

12pt-This is an example of twelve point type.

14pt-This is an example of fourteen poi

18pt-This is an example of eigh

24pt-This is an exampl

30pt-This is an exa

36pt-This is an

better"? Not at all. Too much leading can make the typeset words or lines so "airy" that they seem totally disconnected and float away from each other. The key to determining the amount of leading to be used is the point size itself: 6 points of lead would be too much between address lines under 14 points but might be necessary for legibility when setting three related lines of 36 point. Here again, the best way to illustrate leading and its effect on typeset matter is to show you a few samples:

Our goal has always been to provide a creative professional service at competitive prices. We feel we have succeeded in offering you the experience and insight of a large advertising agency, but with all of the personal attention which only a small art department can provide. We would appreciate a chance to bid on your next bro

Our goal has always been to provide a creative professional service at competitive prices. We feel we have succeeded in offering you the experience and insight of a large advertising agency, but with all of the personal attention which only a small art department can provide. We would appreciate a chance to bid on your next bro

Our goal has always been to provide a creative professional service at competitive prices. We feel we have succeeded in offering you the experience and insight of a large advertising agency, but with all of the personal attention which only a small art department can provide. We would appreciate a chance to bid on your next bro

Top: type set 8/8 (set solid); middle: type set 8/10; bottom: type set 8/16.

Lengthy copy (more than a paragraph) is usually set in upper and lower case; *i.e.*, each sentence begins with a capital letter. A word or two within the text might be set in all capital letters for emphasis (but more often such word or words are set in boldface or italics). Rarely does copy appear all in upper case (capitals).

Letterheads, business cards, and envelopes allow quite a bit of flexibility. Available space (lower case letters take less room than capitals), balance, and emphasis are the determining factors. The three pieces completed for Protektite, Inc. demonstrate the mix of

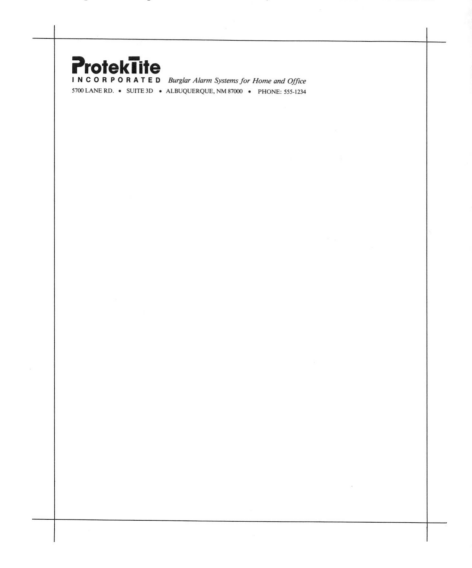

ProtekTite

INCORPORATED *Burglar Alarm Systems for Home and Office*

5700 LANE RD. • SUITE 3D • ALBUQUERQUE, NM 87000 • PHONE: 555-1234

Protek Tite
INCORPORATED
5700 LANE RD. • SUITE 3D
ALBUQUERQUE, NM 87000

Protek Tite   555-1234
INCORPORATED

Burglar Alarm Systems
for Home and Office

5700 Lane Rd. Suite 3D   **John Green**
Albuquerque, NM 87000   President

upper and lower case, as well as the use of just one typeface with several family members to add interest. In the last chapter, I mentioned that it's never a question of right or wrong. The finished work for Protektite, Inc. is by no means the only way it could have looked. Another artist might have come up with a different logo design, choice of type, use of upper-lower, etc. The approach and the finished product are as individual as the creator.

I promised, in the last chapter, to explain how one could refer to typefaces or typestyles as feminine, masculine, or neuter. I've already indicated that body copy is, or should be, neutral (neuter)—the letters of the alphabet formed simply, with no unusual "attention-getters."

Now look at the samples of type on the next page and see if you can tell me their gender. If you are as creative as I think you are, you won't need a lecture on whys and wherefores. Which type might work well in a logo for a women's beauty salon? A sewer and septic tank company? A secretarial service? A boutique? a janitorial service?

There are no absolutes when it comes to making these choices, and the concept is offered only as a starting point—a place to start *thinking*.

CERTAIN FACES SHOULD
NEVER BE SET IN ALL CAPS.

CERTAIN FACES SHOULD
NEVER BE SET IN ALL

CERTAIN FACES
SHOULD NEVER BE SET

I chose the four typestyles in the left column as examples of masculine type. The center column, I feel, are rather feminine typestyles. Type that could be either neuter, used commonly for setting text, is shown in the right column.

One last point concerns the use of capital letters for logo design and large headlines—anyplace calling for distinctive type. Many typefaces were designed, I'm sure, with *initial caps only* in mind, referring to the first letters of each *word* in a sentence. A headline might read, "Brand X Contains More Fiber!" The B, X, C, M, and F are the first letters of each word in the sentence and are, therefore, initial caps.

When capital letters of a typeface are highly designed and very distinctive, they become somewhat illegible when set together. Script is *always* set all lower case (except for the beginning of a sentence) or initial caps only. In the illustration the same phrase has been set in all capital letters in several typefaces. Can you see the difference in legibility?

Whether or not you ever try your hand at typesetting, as a graphic artist you will be dealing with type. These few pointers may come in handy as you begin your career.

Chapter VII

The Camera: Preparation of Photos/Illustrations

Have you ever used a camera to take pictures of people or events? In your career as a graphic artist you may be called upon to operate a very large professional camera to reproduce a component prior to pasteup.

Agencies and printer art departments often have such a camera available to make their paper photographic copies, called *stats* or *PMTs* (photomechanical transfers). The camera can produce an enlarged copy, a reduced copy, or one of the same size as the original. (This camera is not to be confused with the many copying machines such as Xerox that use heat and a toner to reproduce an image.)

When I was introduced to my first professional camera, its physical size and the number of push buttons, doors, dials, and cranks overwhelmed me. I was scared to death. There was no way I could be convinced that this monster was similar in operation to my hand-held 35mm camera. Taking it one step at a time, though, I found that it was: One setting controlled exposure time, another the F-stop, and there were adjustments for proper focus. There were differences, of course: Instead of simply pointing a camera at the subject, one had a copyboard that opened and closed (to secure the "subject") and could be cranked up or down. An awesome set of bellows, for lens extension or retraction, made possible enlargement or reduction. Sheets of paper negative, instead of film, were used and held in place with suction from a vacuum pump.

The cloak-and-dagger feeling I got when working in a darkroom, lit only with eerie red light, took a while to get over. Doing my own camerawork, however, helped me to understand what the printer would or would not be able to do when negatives (film) of the finished artwork (mechanicals) were shot. For that reason, whether or not you get hands-on experience with a commercial camera, it is wise to have a little knowledge about what it will or won't "see." You also need to know how to communicate with the cameraperson (in case it isn't you) and how to mark your various components.

Let's talk a little "camera language." You have a pen-and-ink line drawing of a woman dialing a telephone. Your customer has provided it for use on his flyer but wants it back. This necessitates making a copy—Xerox quality won't do, and a PMT must be made. It will fit the layout without enlarging or reducing. How will you mark this illustration (for your own information or for the cameraperson who will be doing it)? When the original and the copy are to be the same size, a tag can be marked *s/s* (same size) or *100%* (meaning that the copy is to be 100% of the original size).

Another customer, a realtor, needs a particular association logo for her business card. Your file of often-used logos contains the one she needs, but it's much too large. You measure the original and find that it is 1″ square. The logo needs to be ½″ square—or half the size of the original. How's your math? If same size is 100%, what is half? You're correct if you said "50%". Now, if the customer wanted that logo to appear on a brochure in a larger size —say, 2″ square—what should the tag be marked? *Twice* the size of the original (1″ square), or 200%.

Those were easy examples that could be done in your head. But what would you do with a layout that needed a 1¼″ tall drawing of a candle, and all you could find was one that measured 3⅞″? You know, immediately, that the drawing has to be reduced to fit your layout. Also, if you're sharp you'll notice that 4 reduced to 1 (approximately) will be ¼ of the original size, or 25%—but only *approximately*. Usually the size is critical and must be *exact*. Luckily, we don't have t fill two sheets of paper with math computations—we have the proportional scale, often called the *wheel*.

An inner ring of numbers, expressed in inches, is marked "size of original." This inner ring can be turned to line up with a number, also expressed in inches, on an outer ring marked "reproduction size," *i.e.*, finished size desired. A window, with numbers read as percentages, has been cut for viewing toward the top of the inner ring. Going back to the problem of the candle drawing that measures 3⅞" and needs to be reduced to 1¼", we use the wheel and find that the *exact* reduction is 32% (of original size). If the space on the layout had been critical, our guess of 25% would have made a big difference.

Perhaps it goes without saying, but I'd better mention another important consideration: When measuring for enlargement or reduction, the camera works with both vertical and horizontal measurements proportionately. You cannot reduce or enlarge the height/depth (vertical) without a simultaneous, proportionate reduction in width (horizontal). At 50% of original size, an 11" × 17" piece would measure 5½" × 8½"; 8½" × 11" would become 4¼" × 5½". Forgetting to check the final size for both measurements with the wheel can sometimes lead to grief. Let's suppose that the candle drawing measured 2" horizontally. Your layout left a 1¼" square—at 32%, the *width* is reduced to 65/100 of an inch. The drawing might appear too "skinny" to fit the layout comfortably.

Many of the pieces you will put together as a graphic artist will have photographs supplied by the customer. More than likely they will be of assorted shapes and sizes and in horizontal and vertical formats. Perhaps you've done a stunning layout before receiving the photographs. Your layout calls for predominantly vertical photos, but the customer has several that have been taken horizontally. What do you do? Change your whole layout? That might not be necessary with careful *cropping*. Usually photos (taken by other than a professional) have extraneous background material that adds nothing to what the picture is trying to show. A horizontal picture with judicious cropping can be transformed into a square—and with some additional cropping into a vertical picture to fit your layout.

Never mark on or cut the photograph that the customer has supplied. Paper is placed around all four edges for your crop marks. After careful measurement, crop marks are placed to indicate the portion of the picture to be printed. The rest of the picture "doesn't exist." The percentage of enlargement or reduction pertains to the area *inside* your four crop marks only. The customer's photo can be returned intact after printing and removal of the paper containing the crop marks.

For any photograph to be printed, it must be broken down into a pattern of dots (a halftone). A camera cannot handle the color gray—it doesn't "see" it very well. A black-and-white photograph has grays ranging from almost-white to almost-black. Without making it into a halftone, the lightest grays would appear as blank white and the darker grays would be either solid black or an ill-defined smudged area. When converted, the lightest areas of the photo have the lightest dot pattern, and the concentration increases as the picture goes from gray to black.

Halftones are usually shot by the printer's cameraperson preparatory to printing. The screens available and the negative film used produce high-quality reproductions. Occasionally, however, a customer has a low-budget piece and compromises quality for the lower cost of a halftone PMT. If the agency or printer art department where you're employed has a camera and screens, you may be asked to make this *paper* halftone.

What about colored photographs? A customer gives you five photographs to use in a brochure, but one of them is in full color. The halftones in the brochure are to be printed in black and white only. Can you use the colored picture? That depends on your knowledge of what the camera (and, of course, the film) will "see."

Your eye can easily distinguish between red and black, for instance. The camera cannot. Pale yellow, light blue, and white have no similarity to you, but the camera judges them to be nearly the same. Other colors are more dependent on their *value*—light to dark. A man wearing dark brown slacks and a red sweater and leaning against a black car would not photograph well in black and white—especially on a cloudy day. Light is also a variable; artificial light or sunlight can change the value of colors, thereby allowing some differentiation between the man's red sweater and his black car.

On the subject of colored photographs, at times a customer will want pictures *printed* in full color. As we have seen, all photos must be made into halftones before printing. Photos that will also print in color require a special process called *color separation.*

After the photos are marked with the size desired (in inches, rather than percentages), they are sent out to be electronically separated. All full-color photographs (or illustrations) are printed from four negatives: one yellow, one cyan (a shade of blue), one magenta (a shade of red), and one black. The amount of yellow in the phottgraph is translated into a series of dots, just as in a black and white halftone. Orange is obtained when the red dots print over the yellow dots; green is printed when blue dots overlie the yellow dots, and so on. The average person is unaware that the colored pictures in a favorite magazine are nothing but a bunch of dots! Were *you* aware of it? If not, find a magnifying glass and see for yourself! With good magnification, you ought to be able to pick out dots in all four colors: yellow, magenta, cyan, and black.

Let's talk for a moment about illustrations and drawings. If the drawing or illustration is rendered in black ink and composed of lines or dots, a *line shot* is all that is necessary; it doesn't have to be made into a halftone. However, *pencil* drawings or illustrations in shades of gray *wash* cannot be printed without first being converted into halftones. A full-color painting must, like a colored photograph, be sent out for a color separation.

Perhaps YOU have been asked to do a pen-and-ink line drawing for a brochure. You need to sketch it quickly before working in ink. Can you sketch in lead pencil, trace over it in ink, and erase the pencil later? I wouldn't, because even a light residue from the lead pencil wil be "seen" by the camera. You have two choices: Use a light table to trace over the lead pencil sketch (with a clean sheet of paper on top, of course), or do your preliminary drawing with a non-repro blue pencil. The negative film or paper used in most commercial-use cameras is not sensitive to blue, so that a very light blue "drops out" of the picture being shot. If you are not too heavy-handed with your sketching, the blue will not be there when the PMT of your drawing is developed. Please note that I said "light blue"—here, again, *value* is important. Although the film is not sensitive to blue, *navy* blue might be seen as black.

Drawings and illustrations that come from preprinted art services, generically called *clip art,* are prepared correctly for line shot use. The same drawing/illustration is usually supplied in several sizes, but you may find you need a particular one much smaller or larger. If so, watch out for screens. If you must drastically reduce a piece of clip art that is fully or partially screened, you may be in trouble. What happens when the illustration is reduced? The dots become closer together. If the dots are *too* close together the area may photograph as though it were black. When you enlarge, the dots will become further apart. Take that into consideration, also.

Your understanding of what the camera sees will help you explain to a customer why a particular piece of art might not reproduce very well. When you are brought a logo clipped from the Yellow Pages, for instance, you can point out that the camera will also pick up the faint printing from the back of the page. And when another customer brings in a printed business card for minor changes (the original artwork has been lost), you immediately notice that the card is red with black ink. Knowing that red photographs as black, you can tell the customer why you can't simply shoot this card and make the necessary changes—the PMT will be a solid black blob! Customers aren't expected to understand the workings of a camera, but you are.

In the next chapter, Pasteup, we discuss a few more items the all-seeing camera will pick up if you're not careful. Printers respect a graphic artist who is totally professional and makes their work a little easier. Knowledge of the camera, proper communication, and attention to detail will gain you that respect.

Chapter **VIII**

Pasteup

Mrs. Jones and Mrs. Smith of Rainbo-tique would like you to do camera-ready art for a small hand-out flyer announcing their Grand Opening. A printer has given them an excellent price on 3,000 flyers (printed one side, black ink on colored stock) if they will have the artwork prepared 2-up on an $8\frac{1}{2}''$ × $11''$ sheet (making the finished size of the flyer either $4\frac{1}{4}''$ × $11''$ or $8\frac{1}{2}''$ × $5\frac{1}{2}''$). The artwork is also to be used for a 2-column newspaper ad. Before the art is sent to the printer, it can be sized for a reduction and a PMT made to send to the newspaper. The clients have provided an illustration and a very rough layout that may be changed as deemed necessary. The rough shows that Mrs. Jones and Mrs. Smith envision their flyer as $5\frac{1}{2}''$ in width and $8\frac{1}{2}''$ in depth (horizontal measurements are usually quoted first).

The components you'll be working with, then, are: (1) a large heading, "Grand Opening"; (2) fashion illustration; (3) small blocks of copy (to be typeset from their typewritten copy); and (4) logo.

You quickly decide to change one feature of the layout; they have placed the illustration to the right of the main copy block. The figure's face is looking to the right, and thus *off* the page. By switching the placement of illustration and copy, the figure faces *into* the ad (and even appears to be looking at the copy). Though not a hard-and-fast rule, a person or people in a drawing or photo are usually placed looking *into* the page.

After speccing the type and sending it to the typesetter, you're ready to prepare the *artboard*. The use of the word "board" is a little misleading—you're not working with wood! Perhaps it is

Shown greatly reduced.

called board to distinguish it from paper, which is normally quite thin. Artboard ranges from a lightweight bristol (heavier than most papers but still flexible and easily bent) to a ¼″ thick illustration board (very rigid—also very expensive). The printers that I've dealt with through the years dislike the heaviest illustration board because it's difficult for their cameraperson to close the glass door of the copyboard over it. As an employee you will use, of course, whatever is supplied. As a free-lancer, the choice is yours. We'll use, in this case, a 10-ply bristol with a smooth (plate, or hot-press) finish. The finished artwork will be 11″ × 8½″ (2-up, each flyer is half this area), so you need a piece of bristol that is slightly larger, for placement of crop marks. A 12″ × 10″ piece will be adequate.

The first task is to secure the bristol to the drawing board. Your drawing board (or table) is equipped with a T-square or a parallel bar for ruling or pasting up anything horizontal. You place the bristol with the 12″ side lined up horizontally against the parallel bar or T-square. Masking tape at all four corners of the bristol should be enough to keep the art in place as you work, but a little extra tape along the top and bottom edge at center will be insurance. Masking tape, rather than a cellophane tape, is used because it won't tear the artboard when the tape is removed.

Now you are ready to indicate the image areas and component placement with your non-repro blue pencil. Earlier I mentioned printing considerations when doing pasteup. The flyer will be printed on an offset press, and the printing plate has an area where it attaches to the press that will not print at all. This blank area is called *gripper* (the press *grips* the printing plate). There's no reason to list all the press sizes, paper sizes, and gripper requirements that you might encounter. Just know that a printer does require gripper, and when preparing camera-ready art that must be taken into consideration. Leaving gripper space is not a problem with most pieces because photos, illustrations, and copy seldom are placed right to the outer edges of the printed piece.

The Rainbo-tique flyer, printed on a small press, requires ⁵⁄₁₆″ space along the 8½″ edge for gripper. This will not be a problem, because none of the components will be placed that close to any edge. But to be on the safe side it is always wise to lightly rule the *maximum* image area (the area that will print and must contain all your components). Because the final art calls for 2-up, you need an extra set of crop marks to show the printer where to cut the flyers apart. Thus far, what you have ruled out should look like the example on p. 94 (I've added measurements, and your light blue rules are indicated by dotted lines. This is the maximum image area. The pasteup can occupy much less space with no problem— it just cannot exceed the area shown).

Looking at the layout provided, now you lightly sketch (with

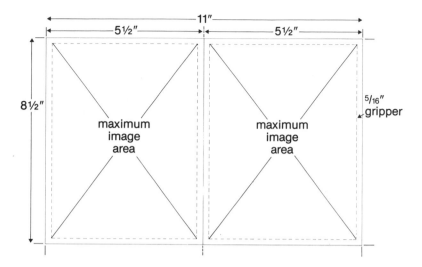

blue pencil) the approximate placement of the components. The heading will be placed on a gentle curve, which you indicate. The typesetter is not able to curve the letters on the machine, so you will have to do it by hand.

Check your equipment before the type arrives: Do you have everything you'll need to work with? You'll need: a triangle, a knife, a ruler or pica pole, a metal edge to cut against, an adhesive, solvent, and a·burnisher.

The triangle is used to line up vertically. With the base of the triangle on the T-square or parallel bar, one side of it is perpendicular. You will have copy for Rainbo-tique that is flush on at least one side. The triangle, placed against that flush edge of the copy, will let you know whether or not the copy has been lined up correctly.

A knife, rather than scissors, is handier to cut lines or blocks of copy out of the galley. If the galley has had adhesive applied on the blank side, scissors become gummed up quickly. Knife blades can be changed easily. My favorite is an X-acto knife with a #11 blade.

Ruler or pica pole? A pica pole *is* a ruler, with measurements in picas as well as inches. But not all rulers are pica poles. A pica pole is normally a 12″ metal rule, but a pica ruler can be purchased that has increments up to 24″ or more. It's handy to have the 12″ pica pole on the drawing board at all times and access to a larger pica ruler for boarding large pieces. The metal edge of the pica pole can be used to cut against. Cutting against most triangles (usually some form of plastic) will ruin them.

Agencies and printer art departments vary on the adhesive used. As an employee you might use rubber cement (purchased in large cans, then poured into individual glass jars with brush), an aerosol spray cement, or wax. Through the years, working for many firms, I've used them all.

Wax is very clean, and copy can be moved easily if the artist changes his/her mind about placement. Its biggest drawback is its sensitivity to heat and cold. If the pasteup is exposed to excessive heat the wax will bleed through the type, discoloring the copy. Too much cold and a word or line of copy may pop off the board.

Aerosol spray cement is expensive, wasteful (hard to eliminate overspray), and, without adequate ventilation, hazardous to your health. At times it is the only adhesive that can be used because it leaves the thinnest and most even coating.

Regular rubber cement is probably the most popular adhesive used. It is a bit time-consuming to work with, however, as two surfaces must be coated: the component and the spot on the board where it is placed. There is no chance that parts of the pasteup will come unglued—with two coats, the copy is there to stay! Unfortunately, once the components have been put down and burnished, changing your mind about placement creates a problem. Peeling up a word, line, or block or copy is nearly impossible. Liberal flooding with solvent is the only thing that works well and will not damage the type. Nor is rubber cement particularly clean. Excess rubber cement seems to get everywhere, no matter how careful you are. However, clean-up with a rubber-cement pickup or the solvent Bestine is easy.

Another rubber-cement adhesive called One Coat has been my choice for quite a while. As its name implies, only one surface needs to be coated, which saves time in pasteup. It has some of the same problems as regular rubber cement, however. As far as repositioning copy is concerned, the best advice is, "Don't burnish until you're sure of component placement."

A burnishing tool is a simple device, pencil size, with a flared bone or plastic surface at one end. The wide, smooth expanse is used to press the type down tightly to the board, eliminating any air bubbles that might be trapped. A small roller with a handle is also used for burnishing.

The type has come back from the typesetter and you're ready to paste up the Grand Opening flyer. The best way to work is from top to bottom so that your T-square or parallel bar won't be constantly sliding over components already placed.

You can cut the type from the galley first and then apply adhesive to the back. But I recommend coating the entire back of the galley first, for two reasons: (1) less chance of slippage as you cut, and (2) difficulty of coating small sections of type. In either case, you need a separate work area for the coating and cutting. Drawing boards are often large enough to have space to the right of the parallel bar or beyond the reach of the T-square. If the entire board has been covered with Borco, this area can be used for coating and cutting. It must be cleaned with solvent regularly (say, between jobs). If the board is too small, a portable work area is needed: (1) any rigid material, covered with Borco or a heavy plastic (the plastic may have to be replaced from time to time); or (2) a pane of glass thick enough to take the pressure of cutting. Glass works well but dulls knife blades very quickly.

Until you become proficient with the knife, it is risky to cut copy from the galley freehand. Line up your cut using a metal edge, staying a minimum of $\frac{1}{16}''$ away from the type, and cut against the edge. Freehand cuts can result in slicing through the type. The all-seeing camera, believe me, will notice your repair job!

Speaking of the camera, I said that there were other things the camera could detect, and I've just mentioned one. Staying $\frac{1}{16}''$ minimum away from the type is important, not only to avoid slicing through the type, but because the edges of the pasted down copy blocks may create a detectable shadow. When the negative is developed, a definite line may be seen surrounding the copy block. The cameraperson must opaque to eliminate that line. If the line is too close to the typeset copy, the opaquer will have difficulty.

Whenever possible, stay ⅛″, ¼″, or more from the copy with your cut. The chapter on Typesetting mentioned the illegibility of type that is set solid; cutting is also a problem. Cutting between lines that are set solid can be a nightmare for the artist *and* the opaquer.

Starting at the top of the pasteup, now, the first typeset copy block reads "HELP US CELEBRATE OUR." This can be cut from the galley and positioned. The parallel bar or T-square is then pushed up to the baseline of the longest word (or line). Look carefully to see that all the letters abut the top edge of the bar or T-square. If some of the letters disappear or run uphill, the copy block isn't properly aligned. If the copy has been positioned very lightly (not burnished), you still have some maneuverability. Even when the copy has been lined up satisfactorily, it's not ready to be burnished. There's always the possibility that you'll want to shift it up, down, left, or right after all the components have been pasted in position.

The words "Grand Opening" require special handling to fit the gentle convex curve. After separating the type from the galley, make a cut between each letter, starting at the top of the letter and stopping just short of the baseline (a concave curve would be done in a reverse manner). You now have a flexible line of type that can follow your layout. The line, when cut and spread, should look like the example below. Note that the cuts are made in the center of the space between the letters, to avoid nicking a letter accidentally.

Again, position very lightly in case an adjustment is desired later. You can't, of course, line this type up. It's a case of "by eye"

judgment. Either the illustration or the block of copy is handled next.

Let's place the fashion drawing. The figure is standing. The only "line up" you can do is vertical. With the edge of your triangle in the approximate center of the figure (you should be able to see through the triangle), see if the amount of shoulders and torso are equal on both sides. Does her spine appear to be vertical? If so, she's probably not about to lose her balance and tip over. Don't burnish. She, too, may need to move up, down, left, or right.

The copy block that is to be placed to the figure's right has been set flush right, ragged left. After lightly positioning the block, there are two line-up procedures. Sliding the vertical edge of your triangle to the flush right edge of the copy, look for letters that are "hanging out" from the triangle's edge. If the copy is perfectly aligned vertically, then doublecheck the baseline of any sentence with the parallel bar or T-square. If one is perfect, the other should be. I'll say it one last time (and this also applies to the remaining components)—don't burnish yet.

The few remaining lines of copy and the logo can now be positioned and lined up in the same manner—checking both vertically and horizontally where possible. The pasteup is almost finished. *Now* is the time to look at it as a whole entity. Is it well balanced? Do the components lead the eye from one to the next in a logical, organized manner? How about the use of air (white space)? If the components are jammed together it may be difficult to tell where one ends and another begins. Just as a period after a sentence or a new paragraph tells a reader that another thought is beginning, white space is used to separate dissimilar components. However, too much white space can also be a problem, especially between *related* components—for instance, a logo and address lines, or "HELP US CELEBRATE OUR" and "Grand Opening." White space automatically says to the eye, "Pause a moment before continuing." If the components are part of the same thought, you don't want one of them drifting off into outer space. So look at the pasteup for use of white space. There are no specific measurements, no rules to go by—just your artistic judgment and keen eye.

How does it look? This is your last chance to move a component

HELP US CELEBRATE OUR

Grand Opening

AND RECEIVE A FREE JEWELRY GIFT WITH ANY PURCHASE!

See our exciting MIZ® line for the "Gal on the Go" . . . Choose separates in bright, bold and sassy solids, stripes or plaids. Take home your *COMPLIMENTARY* color-coordinated designer bracelet with any purchase.

Suit yourself for any occasion with a Mr. K® pantsuit or jumpsuit. Cotton or wool-blend designer fashions for daytime, sleek silks, satins or Celanese for evening. Choose your complimentary accessory with any purchase: choice of silk neck scarf, beaded belt, bracelet or earrings.

SATURDAY NOV. 4 ONLY!

Rainbo-tique

800 7th Street NW • Albuquerque, NM 87000
MONDAY - SATURDAY 10:00 - 6:00

for better balance or more pleasing use of white space. Satisfied? Okay, *now* you can burnish all the components so that they won't pop off the board when it is transported to the printer. Cover the pasteup with clean paper (it needn't be taped down) and, using a burnishing tool, go over everything, paying particular attention to edges and corners. After burnishing, check your work for any adhesive residue and gently remove it with a rubber cement pickup or solvent (just a little bit on a clean cloth or tissue).

There's the completed Grand Opening flyer. You'll now make one one PMT at 100% (same size) for the 2-up presentation and another one, at a reduction, for the newspaper ad.

The finished 2-up mechanical needs to be protected with a taped-on cover. Any blank stock will serve, but tissue paper or an inexpensive tracing paper is often used. If a copy machine isn't used to provide a copy for cusomter proofing, the tissue or tracing paper cover serves another purpose—the customer can read through the cover, and corrections can be noted right where they occur.

A tissue paper or tracing paper cover is also used for color breaks. The Rainbo-tique flyer is to be printed in one color (black) only, but let's suppose it is a two-color piece—black and red. Perhaps the customer wants "Grand Opening" printed in red ink, with everything else in black. Those words are not touching any of the other components, so the printer can make the necessary separation without an overlay being provided by the artist. All the printer needs is an indication, on the tissue or tracing paper, of where the red is to go. Tracing over the words "Grand Opening" with a red pencil is all that is needed (I wouldn't advise a red *marker*, which might bleed through to the work underneath).

The printer does need an overlay, however, if the fashion figure's outfit is to be printed in red (either solid or screened). Registration marks are first placed on the artboard, *outside* the crop marks; three or four are enough, placed at the top, bottom, and at least one side. Preprinted registration marks, consisting of cross hairs inside a circle, are available in rolls, rub-on sheets, or cut-out sheets.

A piece of rubylith or amberlith is then cut and attached securely to the top of the artboard (it should be just a bit smaller than the board). Be careful that the tape doesn't cover any crop marks. Cut lightly with your knife along the perimeter of the figure's clothing, staying in the center of the black ink lines. The amberlith (or rubylith) can now be peeled from its plasticized backing by inserting the knife blade (held as flat as possible) between the film and backing. Scraping the amberlith (well away from where you've cut) may be necessary to get it started. Leave the film on the clothing, removing the rest from its backing. You now have an overlay for the red clothing.

Place another set of registration marks on the overlay directly over those on the base art. The cross hairs in the circle should match exactly. If the overlay becomes detached from the base art, it can be reattached by lining up the two sets of registration marks.

You've done design/layout, type speccing, camerawork, and pasteup now. Are you ready to find employment?

Part 3

Chapter IX

Your Résumé

I stumbled along for many years, early in my career as a graphic artist, without a résumé. I filled out numerous application blanks, trying desperately to remember places, addresses, dates of employment, and supervisors' names—all in the correct sequence. Once in a while after turning in my application I would realize that I had forgotten something important. Embarrassed, I'd approach the desk and ask for it back. Inserting arrows between two items, I would add the missing information (sometimes in the margin). The result made me look, I'm sure, disorganized and unprofessional.

A résumé, prepared in private and with time for careful thought and correction, can save time and embarrassment when entering the offices of a prospective employer. Undoubtedly you'll still be asked to fill out an application. But with a résumé in front of you, the information asked for in the block "Previous Employment" can be copied, or you can simply write "See Résumé" in that block.

Employment ads in newspapers often end with "Send résumé to..." The company purposely omits a telephone number. Without a résumé, how would you be able to respond to such an ad?

I've convinced you that you need a résumé, right? As a beginning graphic artist you obviously won't have a long employment history, but this section is probably the most important to an employer. If you have no employment history as an artist—you've just graduated from high school or completed courses at college or technical school—what do you put in this section?

You may have overlooked or forgotten something that might be used here. Did you work part time while in school? Did you work summers? Doing what? If the employment was in any way related to the job you are applying for, put it down. Perhaps you clerked in a department store, and the manager found out about your artistic abilities. You had the opportunity to design and letter several posters and a few point-of-purchase placards for the counters during the course of your employment. Your résumé might read:

> *September, 1987–June,1988:* Elkins Variety Store, 2420 Main Street, Chaney, New Mexico. Telephone:555-1299. Contact Mr. Albert Elkins.
> Designed posters and point-of-purchase placards for store. Used combination of calligraphy and preprinted rub-on type to produce finished artwork.

What about the primary duties of waiting on customers and stocking shelves? Those activities are not related to the employment you are seeking. You have told the truth about your work at Elkins but have not included all your duties. Later in your career (after one or two positions as artist), you will probably drop your experience at Elkins from your résumé.

In high school or college did you do any free-lance artwork— especially work for which you were paid? How about that flyer for Uncle Joe's hardware store? Uncle Joe thought it was great, and his customers responded enthusiastically to the week-long sale as a result of your efforts. And then Aunt Evelyn's church group asked if you'd like to design the masthead for a newsletter they were starting up. Your pay was negligible in both cases, but they were legitimate free-lance jobs nonetheless. Your résumé might read:

> *January, 1986–February, 1987:* Free-lance artist. Work included design and pasteup of promotional flyer for Allstate Hardware, Chaney, and newsletter masthead design and pasteup for First Presbyterian Church, Clifford, New Mexico.

When writing your résumé, think back to all of your *related* experiences. With proper wording, they can be included in your first résumé. However, if your employment consisted of dishwashing, baby-sitting, delivering pizzas, and there was not the slightest artistic connection—leave it out! If your prospective employer has advertised for an artist with minimum experience (often phrased "willing to train right person"), he/she is not expecting a long work history. Indeed, two or three totally unrelated jobs might make the employer wonder why you hadn't been seeking work as an artist.

You may have noticed the absence of the word "I" in the résumé paragraphs. Neither one begins, "I designed. . ." The employer presumes it's you that he/she is reading about, and the pronoun "I" is not used.

Education is usually the next section of the résumé. Assuming you're a high school graduate, the name of the school, city, state, and year you graduated should appear on your résumé. If you were on the staff (as artist or production manager) of the high school newspaper or yearbook, this would be the place to mention it *briefly*.

Additional schooling, if any, should be listed in the same manner. If you did not graduate or receive a certificate of completion, give the number of years or semesters you did finish. Your course of study is important if art-related. Several semesters of liberal arts or a major in anthropology would shed on light on your ability as an artist. Artist positions on newspaper or yearbook should be mentioned.

I wrote a weekly column for my college newspaper. Although it wasn't an "artist" position, I included it for years on my résumé because copywriting is a useful and related ability in the graphic arts field. The key word is *related*, so put down any position you held, committee you were on, or accomplishment that might indicate experience a prospective employer could find useful.

Most résumés have a brief (*very* brief) section headed "Personal." This is not a place to bare your soul and tell all your secrets, and it can be left out. I'm not sure why it's ever included, but your "Personal" might read:

PERSONAL: Single, no dependents, good health.

References are part of a résumé, also. Who has known you a long time and can vouch for your good character? Mom and and Dad, of course, but prospective employers would rather you put down someone who is not quite so biased. How about the high school principal? A favorite teacher? The next-door neighbors that you've known for years? I'm sure this will jog your memory and that you can come up with three good references (that's plenty). Make sure you have the correct addresses and phone numbers. If you are being seriously considered for a position, the employer will probably contact one or more of your references. You may, of course, handle the matter by putting down "REFERENCES: Upon request." That may be unwise in your first years, however, because (1) you need to have *something* on that 8½ × 11 piece of paper you're presenting, and (2) it may appear, at this stage of the game, a little "uppity." The "REFERENCES: Upon request" can be saved until your résumé has become so lengthy that there simply isn't room to list them on one sheet of paper.

One sheet of paper. That's what I said. There are exceptions, of course, but few résumés need to take up more then one sheet. At first you'll have no trouble keeping your résumé to one side of one sheet of paper (single-sheet résumés are never typed or printed on both sides). As the years go by, however, and you have worked for more than one employer, confining it to one sheet can be difficult. Perhaps that is why the information is always worded so concisely.

My own employment history goes back to 1955—that's over thirty years to try to squeeze onto one side of one sheet of paper! The résumé, at present, eliminates all employment prior to 1973. Current employment is first, then the list goes back chronologically to 1973. I will continue to eliminate the earliest employment data as I need room, or condense the job descriptions a bit more. Lengthy résumés are not necessary. Keep it short. To the point. Professional.

You might organize the sections of your résumé in the following manner: Employment History, followed by Education, then Personal, and, last, References. At the top of the page, of course, your name, address, and phone number should appear. The phone number is very important. Most employers, if you are the chosen applicant, will try and reach you by phone. You can't stay at home by the phone for twenty-four hours a day, but do have the phone covered. If you are dependably home mornings or afternoons, put "mornings" or "afternoons" in parentheses following your phone number. Check the schedules of other members of the household to see if they are able to take messages when you are away. Nothing is more frustrating to employers than inability to reach the person they've decided to hire. When the applicant can't be reached after two or three attempts, the "second choice" applicant will probably get the position.

In addition to content, legibility of your résumé is important. Leave some space after your name, address, and phone number. Each section of the résumé should be separated by at least one line (an extra carriage return on a typewriter). As your first résumé will hardly be lengthy, you might even leave two or three spaces between sections. Within sections use single space, rather than double space.

If you are using a typewriter, make sure that the keystrokes are clean. Letters filled in with ink are hard to read, are distracting, and signal your prospective employer that you're not fussy about details. Use a fresh ribbon to get the darkest, most even impression possible; your copies will reproduce better, also. A good typewriter and white bond paper is the least expensive approach (I'm taking it for granted that you wouldn't submit a handwritten résumé). Copies can be made from your original, as you need them, for as little (in my town) as five cents each. Copies can be made on colored stock at most of the larger copying places. The cost might be a penny or two more per sheet. A pale gray, beige, or cream stock can enhance the appearance of a résumé.

If you own or have access to a computer and printer, you have a few pluses. With disk storage available, your résumé can be called to the screen and updated easily—no need to retype the entire page when employment changes. Also, your "copy center" is right at your elbow; with a printer, each "copy" is an original.

The nicest looking résumés are those that have been typeset, pasted up, and either copied or printed. For a beginning artist the expense would be prohibitive, however. (Typesetting in my town is $40 to $50 per hour, with a minimum ¼ hour charge. Pasteup is $25 to $35 per hour.) Save the typeset résumé for the time when you're seeking a highly paid position.

Chapter **X**

Your Portfolio

A portfolio is two things: a physical container and the contents of the container. Of the two, the contents are far more important. A prospective employer will not be impressed by a large, plush container with nothing inside. Concern yourself with contents first, then tailor the container to the work inside.

When I was starting out, with a large portfolio from my Art Institute tucked under my arm, I thought "the more, the better." Every assignment I had completed was proudly stuffed into that portfolio. There were charcoal figure drawings, landscapes in watercolor and acrylic, abstract designs in tempera, and a few boards that couldn't be easily categorized—"A Study of Textures," "Study of Light as Seen Through a Prism," etc. I now know that the courses I had struggled through were all "preliminary" courses, designed to teach various disciplines and techniques. Later on, had I continued, there would have been assignments geared to finding employment and, thus, good portfolio pieces.

It still embarrasses me when I think about how naive I was. The prospective employers that I did manage to talk to smiled, said that I had a great deal of talent, thanked me...and that was that. Looking back, I wish that someone had been honest with me and taken a moment to tell me why my portfolio wasn't right for finding employment—with that company or any company. And then just a hint or two about what I did need. I learned—the slow and hard way. An advertising agency hired me as a typist/receptionist, and absorbing all that was going to around me I finally pieced together what the business was all about and what was needed in a successful portfolio.

111

Aspiring artists are still coming out of high school and special-ized training and making the same mistake I did. For years as art director and as agency owner, I had the opportunity to see hundreds of portfolios. Many of them were identical to that one of mine so long ago. And, as a prospective employer, I would smile, tell the applicant he/she had a great deal of talent, say thanks, and then— take the young man or woman on a quick tour of the facilities and make suggestions for redoing the portfolio.

This book is my attempt to take *you* aside and prevent that later embarrassment. If you've read this far, you already understand a little about the nature of the work. You won't, I'm sure, pack your portfolio with paintings and drawings (however excellent) that you've done through the years. The only exception might be applying for a position as an illustrator, and even then the portfolio must be planned as to relevancy. What types of things might you be called upon to illustrate? In what medium would you be working? Answering those questions should make a difference in choosing the contents of your portfolio.

An ad I saw recently in our local paper read: "Wanted: Illustra-tor, proficient with pen, ink and wash. Salary, D.O.E." (depending on experience). The company was a large furniture store with an in-house art department that handled all aspects of its advertising. It would be possible for a talented beginning illustrator to be hired, depending on his/her portfolio. I *know* what that prospective em-ployer will see: at least one or two portfolios full of excellent figure drawings, airbrushed automobiles, or gallery-worthy still lifes in oil or acrylic. Talented though the illustrators may be, the ad is from a *furniture store* and it specified *pen and ink.*

I'm sure you see the point. A cartoonist should have a portfolio full of cartoon drawings and ideas. An illustrator should have drawings geared to the company's needs and the specific job he/she is applying for. A layout/design and pasteup person should have examples of design/layout, pasteup, and finished, printed pieces.

Now that I've shot down the idea of using some of the artwork so carefully saved through the years, where do your portfolio pieces come from?

If you do not plan to attend a college or technical school after high school and you want to find a position doing design/layout/ pasteup, you must depend on free-lance work for your portfolio. The types of work experience mentioned in the discussion of the résumé could provide a good beginning (the flyer for Uncle Joe, the masthead for Aunt Evelyn). Posters and point-of-purchase placards, of course, would be too cumbersome to include in a portfolio, but photos of the finished work can be mounted on a page or two and included.

Whenever possible, show the complete sequence; that is, the layout, the mechanical, and the printed piece. And "more" is never automatically "better." A portfolio with two or three well-done pieces is superior to a one crammed with poor-quality work or totally irrelevant art. "More" is better only when, instead of two or three good pieces, you have a dozen...two dozen. The emphasis, of course, is on the word *good* !

No one has an endless upply of Uncle Joes and Aunt Evelyns. If you really want to be a graphic artist and you know you can do the work, why not start right now preparing for your career? If you have a year or two before graduation from high school, why not spend them building an outstanding portfolio? Business people have business cards. If you are to approach someone, other than Uncle Joe or Aunt Evelyn, do it in a professional manner—with a business card.

Make a small investment in your future right now. Purchase the few supplies you need to get started with the money you were going to spend on a new record, the movies. If you know you can do the work, prove it by designing yourself an eye-catching business card. Don't forget your title—"Free-lance Artist."

When you go to the typesetter to purchase type, express your interest in the operation and your desire to learn more about it. Most business people are proud of their company and willing to show a young person what it's all about. After pasteup, find a printer who will print your cards (minimum of 100) and ask if it might be possible to see the equipment in operation.

Now that you have a printed business card, carry some with you at all times. If you haven't yet approached every friend, relative, and speaking acquaintance about artwork they might need, this would be the time. Let your teachers know of your interest in a career in graphic arts and give them one or two of your cards. They might have a friend or relative who would be willing to let you tackle a flyer. Your business card can provide a network of possible leads to free-lance jobs. What's going on at your school? Will they need tickets for a raffle, the Senior play? Find out who is in charge of ordering these printed pieces and ask if you might handle it. Your friendly printer will advise you how to prepare the artwork for printing. If you are truly creative, you'll create ways in which your services can be used. Deciding what to charge may be difficult at first. An hourly wage (as long as you're not too slow) plus actual cost of materials is probably best. You're building portfolio pieces, remember, so don't be greedy.

We've been talking so far about how to get started without benefit of college, university, or technical school. If you do plan to get further schooling, don't feel that the foregoing was not for you. It's never too early to start working on a portfolio. The knowledge and experience gained in any free-lance work cannot be taken away. If anything, your school courses would be that much easier and your grades higher after a trial-and-error period of learning.

Commercial art courses vary in length and what they offer. If it's design/layout/pasteup that you want, make very sure that you'll get specialized training in those areas. A respected technical/vocational school in my town has an excellent graphic arts course that covers not only design/layout and pasteup, but typesetting and printing as well. The graduates have excellent portfolios composed of completed school assignments. There are layouts, camera-ready mechanicals, and printed pieces—tangible proof that they understand the technical aspects of the work.

Such a school will give you the opportunity to fill a portfolio. Then why do I suggest free-lance work in addition? Not, surely, just to make schoolwork easier and your grades higher, but for a more practical reason—as you gain experience, you also gain *speed*. The more pieces you work on, the faster you will become, and customers always seem to be in a hurry for their work. School assignments won't necessarily prepare you for the time pressures you'll encounter as an employee. I hired two technical school graduates, at different times, and found the same problem: The portfolio was superb, the day-to-day work was accurate and neat, but the lack of experience showed in the time needed to complete a piece of artwork. One employee never gained any speed and was dismissed; the other after three or four months could pace herself with the best. Practice makes perfect—and, also, faster!

Portfolio pieces can also be created on the spot, with a particular position in mind. You see an employment ad in the paper that sounds like you: "Artist wanted. Minimum experience O.K. Will train right person. Southern Grafix, (505) 555-8849." What does this company do? Will your portfolio contain the type of artwork the prospective employer is hoping to see? You'll never know unless you pick up the phone and call. An inquiry into the nature of the company's product or service is helpful; this one puts together speculative ads for phone books, exclusively. They do not produce flyers, brochures, or letterheads for the general public. You make an appointment that is four days away and get to work!

Studying the phone book ads for a guide as to size and usual content, you lay out several ads using fictitious company names, addresses, and phone numbers. Hand-set type is slow (and you haven't much time), so you decide to order the type from a type-setter. When the type comes back, you carefully paste up the ads, put them all on one sheet, and have a PMT made.

This one sheet of ads, if it's well done, may land you the job. Remember the furniture store that needed an illustrator? I'm willing to bet that the applicant who was ultimately hired approached it the same way—spent a day or two doing pen, ink, and wash drawings of living room groupings and bedroom sets. If you don't already have it in your portfolio, *create* it for a specific purpose!

Chapter **XI**

Your Interview

You telephoned in response to a newspaper ad: "Pasteup artist wanted. Minimum 3 months experience. Knowledge of camera helpful." The secretary asked if you had the required experience, to which you replied, "Yes" (based on your free-lance work). She also inquired whether you had a portfolio, and again you answered, "Yes." The appointment was set for tomorrow at 10:00 a.m.

Did you get directions? Is your method of transportation dependable? These may seem like strange questions, but as an employer I often had applicants who arrived fifteen to thirty minutes late for appointments saying, "I couldn't find you" or "My car broke down" or "The bus was late." Believe me, that doesn't make a good first impression.

When making your appointment, don't be ashamed to ask for the nearest cross streets if you're unfamiliar with the area. The person you're talking to *wants* you to arrive and will often tell you the easiest route. Make sure that your car is prepared for the trip. If you will be traveling by bus or train, check the schedule and *don't* take the one that gives you only minutes to spare. Better to arrive a few minutes before the appointment time than a few minutes late.

How will you dress? Even though you know a little about this company (a friend of a friend works there) and have heard that the employees can wear jeans to work, *don't* wear jeans to an interview! It is always better to arrive at an interview slightly overdressed. Although pantsuits for women have been acceptable for quite a while, I still think that a simple dress for a young woman and dress slacks and sport shirt for a young man make a better impression. Suit and tie are not necessary for this position but would never be wrong. And ladies, don't ruin the effect of that nice, simple dress with bare legs; even in the summer, hose are appropriate. Your appearance should be that of a professional. And you will be judged first on your appearance. After all, the employer is summing up how you would fit in with the other employees. It should go without saying that you are freshly showered, shaved, and have clean hair. Nothing ever turned me off to a potential employee more than dirty, stringy hair!

It's the morning of the interview. You know exactly where you are going and have a fresh copy of your résumé and your portfolio arranged perfectly for showing. You're very nervous, of course. Nerves can do the strangest things to people—make them excessively talkative or, conversely, absolutely mute. While you're traveling, tell yourself that you won't talk too much or too little, that you'll try to be natural and to relax. Tell yourself to remember to smile. You may not believe this, but the employer (or person conducting the interview) is probably a little nervous, too!

Checking your watch, you find that you are twelve minutes early. You enter the office, and the secretary looks up questioningly. You might say, "I'm Mary Lewis. I have an appointment with Mr. Frank at 10:00. I'm a few minutes early." And *smile*. Undoubtedly you'll be given an application blank and directed to a place where you can wait those few minutes. If you're a smoker, for heaven's sake don't light up—even if there is an ashtray right next to you! As an applicant, and a smoker, I made that mistake. Just as I lit my cigarette, the employer headed toward me and introduced himself. I stood up and then realized I held a lighted cigarette. It was an awkward moment because I wanted to shake hands but couldn't. He had to stand and wait for me while I attempted to put out the cigarette and collect my belongings.

While you're waiting, resist the impulse to be chatty with the person behind the desk (unless, of course, that person starts the conversation). In most cases a receptionist/secretary is busy, and comments or questions (except those related directly to the application) are not welcomed. Occasionally an employer, trying to decide between two equally qualified applicants, asks for input from the front desk person.

You fill out the application quickly and accurately and give it, along with your résumé, to the person behind the front desk. The interviewer finally comes in, picks up your application and résumé, then looks directly at you. "Miss Lewis?" Don't nod. Say "Yes," smile, and rise. If you are comfortable with shaking hands, do so (if you are Mr. Lewis, you would most certainly do so). "I'm Mr. Frank. Let's go in here." You follow him into a room with a large table and chairs around it, obviously a conference room.

Your portfolio can stay on the floor by your chair for a moment. Most employers or interviewers need a few minutes to glance over your résumé and application before looking at your work. You may be questioned about a particular item on the résumé. "Your experience has all been as a free-lance artist?" or "I see you graduated recently from Clifford Tech School? "This isn't intended as a third degree, nor as disparagement; more than likely Mr. Frank is just familiarizing himself with the facts. A first interview is especially uncomfortable, and the intent of questions or statements can be misinterpreted. A nervous applicant sometimes gets defensive and answers, "Yes, *but...*" Don't do it—don't get defensive. You have to begin somewhere, so there's no need to apologize for your limited experience or that until recently you were in a classroom. Your portfolio (if it's good) will speak for itself.

"Well, let's see what you brought," Mr. Frank suggests (or words to that effect). At this point, you can place the portfolio on the table and open it so that it is right side up to the interviewer. A brief commentary on what is being looked at may be helpful. The first piece you present is the flyer that was done for Uncle Joe. You have the layout, the mechanical, and the printed piece. Your commentary might be: "This is a promotional flyer for Allstate Hardware. I submitted this layout to the customer for approval, prepared the camera-ready art, and suggested the stock and ink colors before printing. The customer had no illustration for the trowel that was on sale, so I also provided the line drawing."

School assignments in the portfolio can be handled in the same way—the employer wants to know, step by step, what *you* did. If it was a class project—a book of poetry, typeset, pasted up, and printed—you may not have layout or mechanicals to show. You might say, "I did the typesetting for pages 10 through 24 and the pasteup on pages 9 through 20 for this class project." An indication of your speed might be helpful here. When you pasted up your pages you noted that you were finishing four or five pages in an hour. Depending on the complexity of the pages, this might be something to mention: "I averaged ten to fifteen minutes per page on the pasteup. The last pages went much faster, so I'm sure my speed will increase with the opportunity to do daily pasteup."

Each item in your portfolio will be looked at. You may be questioned about specifics after your brief commentary. Or the interviewer may go on to the next item. Let the interviewer go at his/her own pace. Don't hurry him/her to the next item or attempt to go back to something already seen. It's hard to remain calm and smiling when you feel like a bug on a pin under a microscope. I sympathize, but all I can say is that with each succeeding interview it becomes easier.

At last the final pieces in your portfolio have been looked at and you can close it up. What happens now? Seldom will you be hired on the spot, so don't expect it. Employment ads always draw a large response, and the company will have perhaps a dozen or more applicants to interview before making a decision. If it *does* happen, consider it rare and remember this for "next time." It's usually difficult in the beginning to assess the results of your interview. As an applicant, I learned that the interview was promising if the potential employer asked questions about particular pieces, made favorable comments on any of the work, chatted a little and volunteered information about the company, wanted to discuss salary and hours, asked about my availability, and offered a tour of the offices. The interview was probably not going to lead to employment if the interviewer went too quickly through the portfolio without questions or comments, made no notes for future reference, and stood up and thanked me, glancing at his/her watch as I closed the portfolio. These are just clues, however, and they're not always accurate.

As an employer, I tried to anticipate the questions an applicant might have about hours, salary, and duties before the interview. An applicant has a right to know what pay he/she will receive, the business hours he/she will be working, and the general nature of the duties he/she will be expected to perform. Some employers state the starting pay in the ad itself, so that later discussion is not necessary.

Salaries for graphic artists span a wide range, depending on the experience of the applicant and the city. With three to six months, experience you can probably expect minimum wage or slightly above. The easiest way to handle the question of salary is on the application, which almost always has a space for "Salary Expected." If you put down "Minimum Wage," that is surely all you'll get. Put down "Open," meaning that you are willing to consider whatever the employer is offering. In that way you won't be limiting your salary if the employer is considering paying higher than you expect. The flip side of that coin is not to put down so high a salary that you eliminate yourself from being considered. Suppose you put $5.00 per hour in the "Salary Expected" blank and the employer was prepared to start an employee at $4.00—you might be automatically eliminated from consideration (and never know why).

The employer/interviewer may bring up the subject of hours, salary, and other benefits during the interview and be quite specific on company policies. Or the interviewer might mention none of this and merely ask, "Well, now, do you have any questions you'd like to ask?"

This could be a good time to ask about salary and benefits, but it might be more tactful to ask a few pertinent questions relating to the nature of the work before broaching the subject of pay. If bad comes to worse and you leave the office without this information, wait until the phone call comes saying that you're hired. At that time you can inquire about hours, starting pay, and so on. If any of the information is unacceptable, you can always thank the employer and turn down the job. It's important to know where you stand before your first day of work. You don't want to find that your first paycheck is much less than you had expected or learn from other employees that raises are almost impossible to get or that you won't be eligible for a vacation until you're old and gray!

You're also entitled to know how long it might be before the employer decides on the successful applicant. Most thoughful employers will say, "We'll be making a decision by next Friday" (or in two weeks, or by the end of the month.) If nothing is said, thank the interviewer for his/her time and ask when a decision will be made. Then try to relax—it's all over and you've done the best that you could do. Use the interim period to take other interviews (if possible), just making sure that your telephone will be answered at all times.

Chapter XII

Your Income

If you have visions of becoming a multimillionaire before reaching age thirty-five, perhaps you should reconsider entering the graphic arts field. Careers do exist in which after four to eight years of formal education you can earn a phenomenal entry-level salary. On the other hand, I know of few careers that depend as heavily on innate talent and still can be started without advanced schooling. When finances permit, a two-year or four-year program of specialized training will enhance and broaden this natural ability and provide a solid base of technical knowledge. But *demonstrated* ability (your portfolio), not the certificate or diploma, remains the key that opens the door to this career. It is still possible to enter the field by the "back door," as I did years ago, by taking a job as receptionist in an advertising agency. You might start as a typist, a proofreader, a "go-fer" (errand person)—these positions (probably at minimum wage or slightly higher) are a form of "schooling" or apprenticeship.

As your knowledge, proficiency, and portfolio pieces increase, so will your earnings. None of the reference material on wages has income breakdowns according to city or state. The figures are shown as national averages and cover a wide salary range. In every case it is stated that the highest incomes are to be found in the largest cities: Los Angeles, New York, Chicago. But before you start saving for your plane ticket to one of these metropolises, consider this: The competition is keener, and the living costs are proportionately higher. It is not necessary to flee your present location; advertising agencies, printers, art studios, newspapers,

123

and other businesses needing graphic artists exist everywhere. Living in or near a medium-sized city (100,000–500,000 population) has an advantage: You are more likely to be a big fish in a little pond than a little fish in a big pond. A few years in a smaller town learning as you earn will prepare you best for that move to the big time.

A rather predictable progression exists in the graphic arts field: artist, assistant art director, art director, and free-lancer (self-employed), or business owner. An entry-level artist will probably do a great deal of layout and pasteup. With experience and demonstrated ability will come more design assignments.

In an art department that has several artists and an art director, an increase in business and the hiring of another artist may promote the "senior" artist to the position of assistant art director. With this title would undoubtedly come a substantial increase in duties and salary. The title indicates a management position and indeed involves managing or directing other artists as well as having increased responsibility for scheduling production and meeting deadlines. Greater customer contact is another possible part of the new job description.

Moving up to art director is the next step, through attrition within the company, or simply self-confidence (backed by knowledge and ability) when applying for a new job. Art directors (in large agencies, in large cities) are well paid, but you had probably better forget the forty-hour workweek. The total end-responsibility to meet customer deadlines is on the shoulders of the art director. If it requires weekend or evening hours so be it, with no complaints (no dedication, no job!).

Unless the art director can become general manager or president of the company, this title would be the final promotion within a particular organization. At this point, many in the field start their own business, either as a free-lancer (working out of their home) or as owner of a business employing others. Not every creative artist is endowed with business acumen and "hustle," and this last step requires both to succeed.

When it comes to specific salaries, remember that the range is wide and the figures reflect individual experience as well as the size of the city:

Artists (beginning, little experience): Minimum wage to $11,000 per year.

Artists (proficient at layout and pasteup): $11,000 to $17,000 per year. With design capabilities and more experience, salary can go as high as $30,000.

Assistant art directors: No specific income range given.

Art director (depending on size of agency): $22,000 to $42,500. One reference source gave a range of $53,000 to $65,000 for art director of a major magazine and as much as $80,000 for an executive art director in advertising.

According to the Bureau of Labor Statistics, in 1984 three out of five graphic and fine artists were self-employed—free-lancers. Free-lance pay varies even more widely. The artist usually has a per hour amount established in his/her own mind and gives the customer an estimate of the total cost of the work (hours to complete work times hourly rate plus expenses). A free-lancer must be keenly aware of his/her working speed to be a good estimator. Knowledge of the cost of materials is also essential.

Some free-lancers avoid the estimation process altogether by simply telling the customer he/she will be charged a certain rate per hour plus materials. Sometimes the rate-per-hour can frighten off a potential customer. Free-lance work that I have done has been charged (mentally) at $25 per hour and an estimate given. I work fast, so the total cost to the customer is not unreasonable. Were I to quote only the $25 per hour rate, the customer would have no way of knowing what the final bill would be.

Free-lancers do not receive fringe benefits such as health insurance, retirement plan, or paid vacation. No state or federal income taxes are deducted from monies received, and social security contributions are not withheld. A free-lancer must be sharp at basic bookkeeping (or hire an accountant) so that monies owed are paid to the proper agencies when due. There is also no guarantee of 40-hour-per-week pay. The free-lancer may spend half or more of his/her time hustling for work, and the time cannot be charged to any particular customer. It's not all gravy. The beginning graphic artist is strongly urged to try free-lancing on a part-time basis while holding onto a full-time job.

Most sources agree that the job market for graphic artists in the advertising field will continue to expand through the mid-1990's.

As I said at the beginning of the chapter, as a graphic artist you're not likely to become a multimillionnaire in your thirties, but with ability and dedication you can certainly build a satisfying career for yourself. The employment outlook is promising and the work is fulfilling and reasonably well compensated—why not see how far your creative ability will take you?

References

The following people and firms were helpful in preparation of this book:

Anita Gates, of Monarch Press.
Careers, Inc., Largo, Florida.
Careers, the Institute for Research.
Chronicle Guidance Publications, Inc., Moravia, New York.

Books consulted include:

College Blue Book, 20th ed., Macmillan Publishing.
Jobs! Robert O. and Anne M. Snelling, Simon & Schuster.
Occupational Outlook, 1986–1987, U.S. Department of Labor.
The College Cost Book, 1986–1987, College Entrance Examination Board.

Index